LEADING CONSCIOUSLY

LEADING CONSCIOUSLY

A Pilgrimage Toward Self-Mastery

DEBASHIS CHATTERJEE

Butterworth-Heinemann

Boston Oxford Johannesburg Melbourne New Delhi Singapore

The publisher offers special discounts on bulk orders of this book.

For information, please contact:

Manager of Special Sales
Butterworth–Heinemann
225 Wildwood Avenue
Woburn, MA 01801-2041
Tel: 617-928-2500
Fax: 617-928-2620

For information on all Butterworth–Heinemann books available,
contact our World Wide Web home page at: http://www.bh.com

10 9 8 7 6 5 4 3 2

Printed in the United States of America

Dedication

I truly believe that fire will be discovered for the second time in the history of human civilization. Only this time the spark will come from within the Self.

Conscious leaders of the new millenium will be the harbingers of this inner spark. To them I owe this labor of love.

Contents

Foreword

It has been almost two years since a thoughtful young professor of management from India visited me at MIT and commented, "What is oldest is often most valuable. When an idea has persisted for thousands of years, we can have some confidence in its truth."

That thoughtful young man, Debashis Chatterjee, has now completed a book, and it is a very great privilege to be able to introduce it.

In this book, Debashis Chatterjee presents and explains diverse threads of ancient wisdom teachings, relating these insights to the challenges of leading contemporary organizations. He does so with remarkable clarity, simplicity, and persuasiveness. Ideas that might otherwise be regarded as hopelessly esoteric or impractical emerge as bedrock notions of what it means to lead and to work together effectively. Time honored philosophic perspectives illuminate why work in one setting evokes passion, imagination, and genuine commitment, while all three are absent in another.

In so doing, I find that this book speaks more directly to the crucial problems which afflict contemporary organizations than most "how to" management nostrums.

"If a person rises to a level of authority that exceeds his virtue, all will suffer," wrote Guanzi, a predecessor of Confucius,

2500 years ago. Is there any reason to think this advice less relevant today than when it was written, especially in era of enterprises which influence the lives of people around the world? How many suffer, both inside organizations and beyond, from abuse of power, from leadership lacking wisdom and deep understanding, from decisions based on shallow, frenzied thinking which nonetheless affect thousands? Was this only a problem of 2500 years ago? Or, are we, if anything, more in need now than ever before of a set of guiding precepts to aid in the formation of leaders, so that power would be in balance with virtue?

If so, why is this problem virtually ignored in all the attention paid to high performance, world-class competition, and leading global enterprises?

I think there are two reasons. First, it is not actually the vision we are following. Balancing power with virtue actually runs counter to our more accepted assumptions that people rise to positions of authority because of their competence, their technical skill, or their proven ability to produce results. In fact, this itself is a rather rosy picture. In point of fact, many rise to positions of power because that is their ambition, because they know how to make impressions, because they are masters at the internal political game playing that dominates most large enterprises. Second, even if we did embrace the vision that power and virtue should go together, we have little idea how to pursue such a vision. We have no agreed upon set of guiding ideas as to what constitutes virtue. We have no shared understanding of how virtue and wisdom develop in a person throughout their life. We all recognize the difference between espousing laudable values and practicing those values. But we have little shared understanding of why one person has developed integrity and another has not.

The result is that many in positions of authority lack the capabilities to truly lead. They are not credible. They do not command genuine respect. They are not committed to serve. They are not continually learning and growing. They are not wise.

As Debashis Chatterjee shows, ancient traditions like those of India and China have something important to contribute to understanding true leadership development. The cultivation of virtue, they believed, followed from the development of consciousness. *Development*, Chatterjee points out, has the same root as *envelope*. Development literally mean "de-enveloping" or opening up. As the human being opens up, their awareness expands to embrace more and more of the complexities of life, the realities of their organization, and the principles of nature. Higher virtues are, at some elemental level, nothing more or less than deeply appreciating laws of nature that enable harmony and functioning of life: see reality as it is (commitment to the truth), take no more than you need (waste not, want not), do not control unnecessarily (hierarchical power should be used only when local solutions are not possible, what 17th Century philosophers called the principle of "subsidiarity"), and balance action with non-action (the power of presence, true listening, and non-intervention).

Internalizing such virtues that does not come from "the outside in," taught to us as moral codes that must be followed blindly. These are virtues that we experience and follow naturally as our consciousness opens up, de-envelops. This constitutes a very different approach to leadership development than practiced in most contemporary organizations. It is neither quick nor simple. It demands deep commitment and disciplined practice. It is no "flavor of the month" management fad, its merits have been proven, literally, over thousands of years.

The implications of this book stretch beyond development of hierarchical leaders. Successful enterprises of the coming millennium may find that leadership is too important to be reserved for a few. Leadership comes in many shapes and sizes, only one type of which concerns people in positions of authority. It is not hyperbole to think of "leadership organizations," organizations of leaders. For the principles and practices of de-enveloping apply to all people.

As more and more managers come to understand the importance of growing people in order to grow an enterprise, there will be increasing interest in more powerful theory and method for developing people. Rather than being a peripheral "HR issue," growing people and aligning their creative capacities is now a strategic imperative, perhaps *the* strategic imperative, for many enterprises. No matter what is done in enterprises it is done by people. The maturity and happiness of those people set the tone and determine the capabilities or limitations of that enterprise. We are leaving an era where great strides were made through developing and applying advanced knowledge in manufacturing, marketing, and finance.

These are now the price of admission to global markets. They no longer afford competitive advantage. We are entering an era, I believe, where world class enterprises will build comparable sophistication in understanding and tapping the intelligence and spirit of human beings. This is why I expect this book to be a landmark in the journey toward cultivating the human side of enterprise. In the increasingly global business environment, it is just a matter of time before Western managers recognize the unique storehouse of practical knowledge about consciousness that resides in eastern cultures, and before their Eastern counterparts rediscover it. Debashis Chatterjee's vision of offering ancient insights in a way that makes them understandable to contemporary managers could not be more timely.

In an era entranced by "the new," our greatest hope ironically my lie in rediscovering "the old." No one has yet been able to improve upon love, nor found a technological substitute for joy, or for serenity. It is not that ancient wisdom is sacrosanct, nor that all answers to life's mysteries were revealed by India's vedic sages. Rather, I see Debashis' most central message as really an invitation. Do we wish to rejoin an ancient line of inquiry? Do we wish to once again focus our energies on understanding what it means to be alive, to be aware, to understand the sources of health and well being, of generativeness, of happiness? If the answer is yes, then it would be foolhardy indeed to ignore the foundations we might build on. They are present in all the great spiritual traditions of the world. But they are in many ways especially accessible in those settings, like India and

China, where there has been some continuity of development, some preservation of not only the articulations of spiritual insight but of the practices as well.

This is a precious book. I hope finds its way into the hands of readers who are as committed to the future as is its author.

Peter M. Senge
Cambridge, Massachusetts
September, 1997

Prelude

This book is not mine. It just came through me. I started writing it one spring morning on the bank of the Mississippi in St. Paul, Minnesota. The first few pages were written in a state of trance. It was as though I was possessed by the spring itself. The words blossomed spontaneously; the script flowed effortlessly like the course of the river through a labyrinth of ideas. And then the writing stopped for a while. The words became frozen. I struggled and gave up, waiting for the next burst of inspiration to come to me. It did come, this time in the middle of summer in the foothills of the Himalayas in India. To the river and to the mountain I owe my journey as a writer.

This book is truly an adventure of consciousness. I would therefore suggest that you read it in the same way that it was written: in silence and in solitude. It contains a rich storehouse of wisdom from the important spiritual traditions of the world. A certain receptivity and quietness of mind is required to come to terms with what the great masters of antiquity and the present are trying to convey to us through their lived lives and their spoken words.

Words are metaphors for real experience. By themselves words mean nothing, but if you can connect your words to your experience, they can set you on course toward a transformational journey. In this journey, words become live channels for the transfer of experience. They serve as spiritual guides for the growth of our consciousness. I recommend that you read the words in this book in the light of your own experience. Perhaps only then will you see how the metaphors trigger a metamorphosis in your consciousness.

I must make it clear that this work is not meant to satisfy the intellectual curiosity of scholars of philosophy, religion, or management. It is a source book for practice. I believe that a principle, however exalted it may be, is as good as dead if it is not proved in practice. The world of consciousness that I am talking about is not a theoretical world of abstract ideas. It is as real a world as anything that you may have encountered so far.

For those of us who are looking for a deeper connectedness with ourselves in life or at work, this book will be of value. I have tried to incorporate my firsthand experience with what I call *actionable spirituality*. In many places around the world where I have spoken about consciousness, people have asked me, is this New Age wisdom? In reply, I have always said, "No, what you hear is on the cutting edge of old age." Never before has the wisdom of the ancients become so relevant as it is today.

We all live in a world of time where the mind finds comfort in pigeonholing experiences into new and old. Let us for once experience that which is timeless; all questions relating to chronology will then disappear. What will remain is the experience.

This book is an invitation to a pilgrimage of self-mastery. I sincerely believe that the self is the beginning and the end of all our journeys, all our experiences. Can we imagine one single moment in our lives in which our self was not with us? Great men and women of great civilizations have undertaken the same journey on which you and I find ourselves. They have left their footprints, memorable milestones of thoughts and actions, to help us travel along. All I have done for you is to collect those timeless footprints from the sands of time.

Leadership is not a privilege of a handful of the high and mighty. It is a state of relationship between the leader and the led. A relationship cannot be possessed by a person; it ceases to be a relationship then. We would recognize that in each follower there is an emerging leader, and leaders can lead because they are connected by this subtle but emergent quality of follower-ship that exists in all of us. Here I have tried to give you, not one model of leadership, but several dimensions of followership that constitute a leader.

Each one of us, consciously or unconsciously, has led in some field or another: as parents, teachers, managers, doctors, athletes, entrepreneurs, or even as students. In all these roles we learn valuable lessons in leadership. I have as well. I remember one of India's greatest men, Rabindranath Tagore, saying that each one of us is the supreme leader in his or her own kingdom. Leadership is not a science or an art, it is a state of consciousness in which we discover the path to our own kingdoms. It is in Tagore's words that I have discovered the highest expression of my pilgrimage toward leadership:

> Where the mind is without fear and the head is held high; Where knowledge is free; Where the world has not been broken up into fragments by narrow domestic walls; Where words come out from the depth of truth; Where tireless striving stretches its arms towards perfection; Where the clear stream of reason has not lost its way into the dreary desert sand of dead habit; Where the mind is led forward into ever-widening thought and action.

May these lines be your stepping stone as you undertake this pilgrimage toward self-mastery. This journey of many miles does indeed begin with a single step.

Acknowledgments

Knowledge is finite. What is infinite is ignorance. After writing this book, I realized how much I did not know about my own self. If I have anything in common with you it is this ignorance. We all share the anatomy of ignorance in some way or the other. Even the wisest of human beings has not been afraid to say, "I do not know."

So I acknowledge, with humility, the many known and unknown sources of the knowledge contained in this book. My parents, my grandmother, my schoolteachers, my spiritual mentors, the sacred soil of India where I grew up, unknown co-travelers on my journeys around the world have all contributed to the unseen dimensions of this book.

First I would like to thank Dr. Peter Senge of the Massachusetts Institute of Technology, who enabled me to dream of this book during my first conversation with him at his learning organization seminar in Cambridge, Massachusetts. This work is an attempt to repay a part of my debt to Peter for all his acts of kindness that opened up a new chapter in my life. What started as a dream turned to reality when Karen Speerstra took me to lunch in a restaurant in Boston to discuss the proposal for this book, which was then cooking in my mind. I wish to thank Karen for her very generous gesture and her patience in supporting this work. I am grateful to Stephanie Gelman, who helped with the editing of the book. I acknowledge the contributions made by Rotary International and the Fulbright Foundation in funding my work in the U.S.

Thank you Jerry Halverson, Michael Naughton, Tom Halloran, Kenneth Goodpaster, Ellen Kennedy, Margaret Lulic, Lee Lawton, and Mary-Jean Loomis in Minnesota for contributing in some way or the other to this book. Nihar Chatterjee of IIM, Calcutta, for your wonderful illustrations. Mr. K. N. Mukherjee for so kindly agreeing to go through the manuscript. Parimal for your long-distance spiritual help. Soumenda and Sanjoy for your love. Mariann for just being there. Ahmed Abdelaal for your Egyptian charm. Dr. Marsha Milburn and Joy for thinking well of me. Rita Cleary and Jean McDonald—my heartfelt gratitude.

Dr. Harsh Muthal for sharing my conviction in a conscious world. Dr. Leo Burke of Motorola, Tom Philips and Carol Rubarts of Ford Motor Company, Sandy Calvert of 3M for your support. Dr. Jan Adams for your words of encouragement. Kanchan in Boston and Kuhan in London, my gratitude for sharing with me your spirits. S.K.C, thank you for your radical teaching without which this "rebellious work" may not have been born. Mr. Swaraj Paul, your gift of love to revive the London Zoo makes you a truly conscious leader: this author wants you to believe that Ambika still lives on to serve a greater purpose. Mother Teresa, thank you for blessing this life and this work.

Finally, Aditi and Shristi, I am lucky to have had you around while this book was being written. This work would be incomplete without you.

His own Self must be conquered by the king for all time; then only are his enemies to be conquered.

…RISHI VYASA, *The Mahabharata*, 1000 B.C.

1

Leadership and Personal Mastery

THE ART OF SEEING

Personal mastery is a function of the quality of our seeing. Great masters in ancient civilizations were known as seers. Those great seers saw nothing magical. The uniqueness of their vision was that they possessed not only sight but also insight. The masters saw the world around them perceptively, not passively. Most of us would look at a falling apple and soon forget about it. It takes a Newton's insight to see through the event and discover the force of gravity. We all see suffering all around us. Yet it takes the insight of a Buddha to go to the root cause of human suffering and identify it as desire.

We are visual ragpickers. In the ordinary state of consciousness, we passively pick up fragmented visual impressions of objects or events. This is a low-energy activity like mechanical picking up of bits and pieces from our environment. High-energy seeing involves not accumulating objects or events but something more. It involves the discipline of seeing through events to the invisible processes that shape those events.

> *Three Zen masters are walking across a field. The youngest among them notices a flag tied to a pole. He draws the attention of his two companions and says, "Look, how the flag moves." The middle-aged master pats the younger one on the back and says, "My boy, can't you see it is not the flag that moves, it is the wind that moves." The old master who had been listening to the other two in silence softly says, "If you have insight, you will see that it is neither the flag nor the wind that moves, it is the mind that moves."*

True seeing is not merely glancing the visible surface of objective reality. True seeing involves perceptive vision of the invisible potential of objective reality.

> *An ordinary salesperson visits an island where nobody wears shoes and says, "You can't sell shoes here. Nobody wears shoes on this island." This is low-energy seeing. Compare this with the high-energy seeing of a market leader who goes to the same island and exclaims: "Look at that! Nobody wears shoes here. What a potential market to get these people to start wearing shoes."*

Seers are therefore not only mystics and sages. They abound in all walks of life—business, politics, science, and sports as well as in religious institutions. Learning to see is the foundation of all disciplines. In India, which is the cradle of the most enduring civilization of the world, the word for seeing is *darshan*. The Sanskrit word *darshan* has more than one meaning. It also means "world view" or "philosophy of life." *Darshan* captures the essence of seeing in its multiple meanings. It lends to the act of passive seeing a quality it lacks—a perspective. Sight as well as insight constitute a perspective. From a clear perspective we get clarity of vision. It is vision that provides guidelines for our actions as leaders.

To see is also to know and to understand with clarity. In the middle of a counseling meeting with a nonperforming employee, a team leader stops for a while and says to the employee, "Oh, now I see your point." In this "seeing" the leader begins truly to understand the follower. This kind of seeing has the same effect as a gentle human touch. High-energy seeing enables you to touch events or persons with the quality of awareness. In this act a certain energy or vitality works between the seer and the seen. There is a subtle communication, a communion between the seer and the seen. When a leader undergoes this communion with her followers, empathy is established. Empathy is the glue, the very substance that enables the leader and the follower to stay together on the same path.

Seeing is not only receiving images on the retina. It is an act of interpretation. Seeing is creative reconstruction of our universe. Leaders are not content with facts. They have immense energy to reorganize facts toward new ideals and newer visions of truth. In day to day life we do not understand the difference between facts and truth. Yet depending on the quality of our seeing, facts and truth emerge as different entities. Facts are frozen forms of truth in a certain space and time. Facts are not the whole truth, although they may contain certain elements of truth. You may take a photograph of the ocean and give us facts about the ocean. But can such a fact encompass the whole truth of the ocean?

Facts may resemble truth in a certain context, but when the context changes, facts also change to accommodate the truth. For example, most people at a certain time in our civilization believed that the earth was as flat as a pancake. Ancient mariners were afraid to sail too far because they feared their ships would topple over to an unknown underworld. This was so because the facts that they saw around them gave them an impression of the flatness of the earth. As soon as a leader was brave enough to take his ship over what was thought to be the edge of the earth, he saw new facts. These facts contradicted the earlier facts, and the earth came to be regarded as a solid round ball. Soon enough, new facts in the shape of photographs of the earth taken from space told us that the earth was not round but that its geometric shape was an oblate spheroid. This meant the earth is less like a ball and more like an orange—slightly flattened at the poles and slightly swollen at the equator. But truth, which has new ways of slipping through our prison of facts, now gives us new facts about our earth. Today's new leader, the quantum physicist, will tell you, "You know, this earth is not solid at all. It is a huge energy soup rippling like a bubble in empty space."

We may therefore say that the quality of our seeing shapes our perspective of truth. When we see with uncreative, low-energy vision we see disconnected facts and often miss the truth. This is because our attention devoid of energy becomes frozen in the outer shell of facts, and truth passes us by. We do exert ourselves in our quest for the inner truth about our many assumptions about life. Most of us remain content with what appears obvious. Reality based on static models or established procedures gives us the security of being a part of the herd. But that reality is not what a conscious leader rests with. It is an insult to her intelligence if a leader is unable to process reality creatively to meet new challenges. As I was glancing through the 1991 annual report of the Coca-Cola Company, a couple of very insightful statements made by Roberto C. Goizueta, the chief executive officer, and Donald R. Keough, then president of the company came to my notice:

> As an organization, we are not wasting our energy forecasting what the future of the soft drink industry will be like in the many countries around the world in which we operate. And neither are we spending our time forecasting what the future holds for this Company. We will use our resources to construct today the foundation of our future. . . . The future we are creating for ourselves . . . will be built.

We don't view the future as preordained, but as an infinite series of openings, of possibilities. What is required to succeed in the middle of this uncertainty is what the Greeks called "practical intelligence." Above all else, this "practical intelligence" forces adaptability and teaches constant preparedness. It acknowledges that nothing succeeds quite as planned, and that the model is not the reality.

The Greek notion of practical intelligence comes from a certain depth of insight conveyed by the Indian word *darshan*. Practical intelligence is a function of integral vision—the ability to integrate sight with insight. *Darshan* penetrates the veil of static models of life and looks at the dynamism of life itself. *Darshan* is the awareness of the depth and magnificence of the moment. When we pay total attention to the reality of the moment, we become one with the moment. The wall between us and reality comes down. We become the reality itself. A great degree of energy is released as a result of our participation with reality. Personal mastery is the embodiment of the energy of this participation. The great Greek philosopher Archimedes expressed this energy as *eureka*, which signified the great triumph of a new discovery.

THE PLAY OF ENERGY

We understand, therefore, that personal mastery is an energy phenomenon. Every action of ours, every gesture, every thought, every intention, every emotion, and even the faintest flicker of our consciousness is a constant play of energy. Whereas the Statue of Liberty and the Taj Mahal are objective manifestations of creative energy, the general theory of relativity and *Paradise Lost* are subjective impressions of the same energy.

When we look at the source of this energy from the point of view of raw materialism, we find that the same molecule of sugar that released the energy for Einstein's conceptualization of the theory of relativity is responsible for Buddha's realization of nirvana as well as Hitler's aggression on the world. Yet we know that merely studying the structure of a sugar molecule will not yield to us the secret of an Einstein, a Buddha, or a Hitler. It is not mere energy but energy combined with awareness that gave birth to those figures of history. Personal mastery comes not from merely accumulating energy but through processing this energy in the light of our awareness. Personal mastery is the science and art of channeling energy from that which we consider purposeless to that we hold as purposeful.

Mastery of our energy therefore lies in bringing the fullness of our being to our task. In simple words, it is the bringing together of the sum total of who we are to what we do. The classical Indian word for energy work is *tapas*. The Japanese have a similar word, *shugyo*. Both *tapas* and *shugyo* imply the discipline of self-mastery. Ancient civilizations understood the importance of cultivation of energy through rigorous discipline. This consisted of being aware of the nature of our energy body. It was the first step toward what the ancients called self-knowledge.

The source of our knowledge about our energy is our being or our self. If we pay attention to the state of our being from time to time, we experience that energy flows through us in a certain pattern. During sunrise the quality of our energy is different from that during sunset. In the morning our energy pushes us to action; in the evening the same energy mellows toward contemplation. We can sense the state of our energy merely by remembering ourselves as a regular discipline. If we practice the discipline of remembering ourselves, we will become amused witnesses to the folly of many of our actions.

> *A busy executive driving toward his office in the morning is caught in a traffic jam. His precious energy, ready to engage itself in the affairs of the work, is boiling over. He knows he cannot move ahead unless the jam eases. Yet the executive honks away like a man possessed. If he had remembered himself during his insane moments of honking, he would have known that he was wasting energy that could be used in productive thinking.*

Many of us fritter away our energies in negative emotions. We become irritable. We are gripped by unpleasant emotions that cause undue tension in our muscles. All of these eat away our vitality. I have often observed people contort their faces and frown during brainstorming sessions. My knowledge about human anatomy tells me that our brains do not have muscles. Yet how much of our energy do we unnecessarily lock into our facial muscles as we "storm our brains"?

Great masters were adept in conserving energy over time only to release it at those precise moments that changed the course of history. Frederich Nietzsche expressed this phenomenon in brilliant language:

> Great men, like great epochs, are explosive material in whom tremendous energy has been accumulated; their prerequisite has always been, historically and physiologically, that a protracted assembling, accumulating, economizing, and preserving has preceded them—that there has been no explosion for a long time.

FROM CAPABILITY TO COPABILITY

Personal mastery is a function of both capability and "copability." When one's self acts on the environment we demonstrate our capability. However, when our environment begins to act on one's self, what is tested is our copability (ability to cope).

> *A bright engineer who was among the several thousand employees who lost her job during downsizing by the telecommunication giant AT&T found out that what mattered during her sudden unemployment was not her capability but her copability. She was still a capable engineer, bright and efficient. But her engineering skills alone were incapable of steering her through the crisis with which the loss of job brought her face to face. In short, what mattered now was how she could cope with the emotional trauma of living with her present condition.*

Our capabilities are measured in terms of our skills in negotiating the outward environment. Capability is the visible, tangible aspect of our competence. It is the outbound energy that shows up as our work, track records of achievements, our credentials, and all that we did to carve out a niche in the environment. On the other hand, copability is the energy that the self gathers together to face an unpredictable environment. It is a discernible niche of experience and expertise in one's inner environment. The mechanism of copability enables the body to shoot out a surge of adrenaline when we face a hostile enemy.

The way we deal with pain and losses also demonstrates our copability. In encountering pain and losses in the context of our life and work-life, we often falter. A man who is unable to get along with his spouse becomes an alcoholic. A fast-track executive misses a promotion and nurtures her sense of loss in the form of an ulcer. When the environment behaves in a manner that seems unpredictable to us, we find it difficult to cope. We fail to realize, however, that the environment "out there" is merely our interpretation of it. If we did not interpret loss of a promotion as the end of the world for us, we would not be so miserable.

To a great extent our copability depends on the way we interpret the reality of our environment. As the top man at Chrysler, Lee Iacocca, then 65 years of age, interpreted the reality of the leader's position in the following words: "The CEO's job is yours to lose." These words were addressed to Gerald Greenwald, who at 54 was then vice-chairman at Chrysler. For Greenwald, Iacocca's words could mean two things: The CEO's job is full of insecurity, and the CEO's job is a constant challenge to perform. Greenwald interpreted Iacocca's words as: "Look, you gotta perform." A financial manager by profession, Greenwald not only enabled Chrysler to stave off bankruptcy in 1979 but also went on to become chief executive officer of United Employees Acquisition Corporation.

Pains and losses are apparent blocks that our environment places before us. We can interpret these blocks as obstacles to our happiness or as greater challenges with which we must cope to receive greater rewards. How then do we enhance our ability to cope? The only way we can do this is to enrich our perspective on what we may at first interpret as "pain" or "lost opportunity" or "a problem." Enriching our perspective on such problems involves a greater depth of perception. This means that we must look at the multidimensional nature of our situations, in which the flip side of a problem is an opportunity. To reinforce what I wrote earlier, it is the quality of our seeing that makes problems look like opportunities.

FROM SELF-IMAGE TO THE REAL SELF

Many of our problems are self-created. The source of self-created problems is the fact that we mistake self-image for our real self.

Self-image is nothing but the accumulated projections of our identity. Self-image is a cluster of names and forms by which we differentiate ourselves from the rest of our environment. We have different self-images as a parent, as a spouse, or as a colleague at work. We perform various roles in various spheres of life. Each of these roles creates a certain impression of our self in our consciousness. Thus one sees oneself as a liberal parent or as a task-oriented boss or as a considerate spouse. All these images of ourselves help us to stabilize our identities in our own eyes.

The problem occurs whenever we confront a reality not consistent with our self-image. For instance, when one receives information from the outside world that one is an autocratic boss, or an uncaring spouse, or an "an ugly fat slob" one's self-image is hurt. We attempt to defend our self-images by various means. We may become angry or indifferent to the outside reality. We may take negative feedback from others too seriously and feel dejected. We may also try to conform to something we imagine to be socially acceptable. All these methods may give us a temporary sense of relief, but they cannot equip us to catch up with the mirage that is our self-image.

Self-image makes us vulnerable to changes outside us. If our self-image is one of an evergreen youth, the appearance of the first gray hair makes us lose sleep. We are traumatized by a single rejection slip from an editor if our self-image is that of a successful writer. Our self-image makes us vulnerable simply because much of this image is unreal. Self-image is a frozen model of our real selves. Just as a model is a symbol or attribute of reality and not the entire reality, one's self-image is merely a projection of the real self. More often than not this projection is a distortion of the real self as a shadow can be distortion of real substance.

How does one go beyond the veil of self-image in search of the real self? The quest for the self can begin only when we have turned our attention from the world outside to the world inside. This is also a transformation in the quality of our seeing: from mere sight to insight. The journey toward self-realization involves the disciplines of silence and solitude. Silence frees us from the noise of our exteriorized consciousness and allows us to probe our inner voice. Solitude enables us to be intimate with ourselves. In deep silence and solitude we begin to glimpse the truth of our lives. We realize that whatever exists is an expression of existence and that our many ways of living are expressions of life itself. We also understand, as the *Bhagavad Gita* tells us: "The unreal has no being: the real never ceases to be. The final truth about them both has thus been perceived by the seers of ultimate reality" (Chapter 2, verse 16). *A Course in Miracles* echoes this truth in saying that which is real cannot be threatened and that which is unreal does not exist.

I have often asked professionals in all walks of life a question very often asked, Who are you? I receive predictable answers like engineer, marketing manager, and ear, nose, and throat specialist. The next question I ask is, Who knows you are all of these? This time the answers revolve around "mind" or "thought." Then I proceed to ask the final clinching question, Who knows you have a mind? This time a silence descends on my audience. In that silence we begin to glimpse the truth of our selves, which is beyond all names and forms.

THE BODY: FOUNDATION OF THE SELF

Conventionally what we know as our body is nothing but an optical illusion. For example, we believe that our bodies are solid structures. But this solidity is a mere appearance. If we could magnify the body to the size of the earth or, better still, invent a microscope that would give us a real look at our bodies, we would find that more than 99.99% of this body is empty space. This space has the same quality and is proportionately as empty as intergalactic space (Chopra, 1989). We can no longer avoid the void that constitutes a large portion of our bodies. This void, however, is not like a deserted land where life stands still. The void is made up of the fullness of our being. It is the source of nonmaterial intelligence that not only sustains our body but also holds together the entire universe. To the discerning eye the human body would appear more like a vibration of energy than a solid material structure.

The Upanishads, the most ancient sacred literature of India, describe the relation between our selves and our universe in delightful poetry:

As is the human body
so is the cosmic body.
As is the human mind
so is the cosmic mind.
As is the microcosm
so is the macrocosm.
As is the atom
so is the universe.

The sages and seers of the Upanishads clearly understood the nature of the human body through sheer experience. The experimental findings of quantum physics at the turn of the century are validating this experience. From the point of view of quantum mechanics, our body would appear less as an object and more as an event in space and time. Quantum physicists describe this body as a local expression of the global field of energy and information.

Another illusion about the body is that it is a closed system—a mere sack of matter separate from the rest of the world. The truth is that with each breath, each of us exchanges several billion atoms with the universe. The skin is a constant medium of exchange between us and our environment. As a matter of fact, the various biorhythms that our bodies experience are localized expressions of the universal rhythms of the cosmos. A sunrise or sunset affects the biochemistry of our bodies. Changes in seasons profoundly affect our moods—we feel dismal in winter and lively in spring. There are no sharp edges between us and our world. In the real sense one's universe is a mere extension of one's body.

Incredible as it may sound, the ancient sages of India had acquired sufficient mastery over their bodies to realize that the organization of the entire universe could be understood by means of simple exploration of the reality of the self. The sages called the universal self the *higher self*, which the physicists of today are attempting to describe as the nonlocal field of awareness, as follows:

In the scheme of nature, you and I are a privileged species. We have a nervous system that is capable of becoming aware of the energy and informational content of that localized field that gives rise to our physical body. We experience the field subjectively as our own thoughts, feelings, emotions, desires, memories, instincts, drives and beliefs. This same field is experienced objectively as the physical body—and through the physical body we experience this field as the world. But it's all the same stuff. That is why the ancient seers exclaimed, "I am that, you are that, all this is that, and that's all there is."

    . . . DEEPAK CHOPRA, *The Seven Spiritual Laws of Success*, 1994

A third illusion we have about the body is that it is a fixed structure that never changes. By convention we also know that we inhabit the same physical body until we die. Although it may be true that the structure of one's body may look the same in a lifetime, we only retain 2 percent of all the atoms in our bodies each year. That is, 98 percent of one's body in 1997 is different from the body it was in 1996. As Dr. Deepak Chopra, a pioneer in the field of medicine, would tell us, we acquire a new liver every six months, a new skeleton every three months, a new skin once a month, and a new stomach lining every five days.

Thus we see that our bodies are open and dynamic patterns of energy and information the apparent rigidity of which mesmerizes us. We feel comfortable in defining our bodies on the basis of certain forms and structures. Yet every definition of the body is illusory—a vain attempt to isolate and fragment ourselves from our universal bodies. Buddha was once asked, "Is the soul one thing and body another?" He said, "That is a matter on which I have expressed no opinion." Great masters clearly saw the futility of limiting the notion of the body. Their mastery was in experiencing the undivided unity of their bodies with the cosmic body.

We can begin to experience the notion of personal mastery in relation to our bodies by paying attention to the following:

1. One's environment does not lie outside one's body. Our bodies are part of what we understand as our environment. Sometimes what we think of as a problem "out there" would not exist if we did not recognize it as a problem "in here." When we are physically unwell, even a bright day can look gloomy.

2. There is no real opposition between our inner and outer realities. The body is merely an intermediary between our inner and outer environments. When a body is fragmented, the entire universe appears fragmented. When a body is whole, the universe appears whole.

3. We are accustomed, by the force of habit, to pay attention to the world outside our bodies. Rarely does our awareness dwell inside. We can cultivate the habit of looking within our bodies by interiorizing our consciousness.

4. One's body is a vast energy field that operates in several layers. These layers manifest themselves from the subtle to the gross. Each layer of energy corresponds to a certain level of awareness. By merely shifting our awareness, we can bring about profound changes in our bodies. Through awareness we can heal ourselves and solve complex psychosomatic (body-mind) problems.

5. The energy of our being (awareness) is more subtle than our energy of thinking. The energy of our thinking is more subtle than the energy of our doing.

6. When one's body is able to integrate several layers of energy into one unity, there is a breakthrough in awareness. When the energy layers in the body are fragmented, there is a breakdown in awareness.

7. A disintegrated body experiences chaos, disease, and sickness. An integrated body experiences cosmos, ease, and health.

In their book *An Unused Intelligence: Physical Thinking for 21st Century Leadership*, Andy Bryner and Dawna Markova vividly describe the problem-solving potential of the body in the context of organizations. They argue that at work we are trained in time management, in negotiation, and in quality procedures, but we are never taught to notice how we are relating physically and energetically to people, events, and contents of our job. This inexperience, the authors point out, pushes us toward unexamined responses at the workplace, such as stances of control, reactivity, rigidity, and opposition. Our ignorance of the untapped intelligence of our bodies leads to wasted human potential, which could otherwise be used creatively. Bryner and Markova write:

> Thinking through our bodies can go a long way toward facilitating the kinds of flexible, creative minds so desperately needed in organizations today. The word "incorporated" gives us this clue in its etymology; it's Latin root *corporare*, means to adopt or form into a body. Incorporating or embodying our business thinking is a dynamic way to explore the path between abstract ideas and implemented action.
>
> . . . ANDY BRYNER AND DAWNA MARKOVA, *An Unused Intelligence: Physical Thinking for 21st Century Leadership*, 1996

Organizational learning based purely on abstract ideas is unlikely to help us solve real-life problems. The participation of the body in problem solving is sometimes as important as the mind's engagement with the context of the problem. The following story illustrates this:

> *A philosopher proud of his knowledge hired an illiterate boatman to ferry him across a wide river. While crossing the turbulent river, the philosopher, unable to restrain his tongue, constantly lectured to the boatman about the nature of existence. He asked the boatman several complicated questions about life and all the while the boatman remained silent.*
> *"Have you never studied grammar?" asked the philosopher.*
> *"No," said the boatman.*
> *"In that case, half your life has been wasted."*
> *The boatman said nothing.*
> *Soon a terrible storm blew up. The boat was tossed about by the wind. The boatman leaned over toward the philosopher.*
> *"Have you ever learned to swim?" asked the boatman.*
> *"No," said the philosopher.*
> *"In that case sir," the boatman retorted, "all your life is lost, because the boat is sinking."*

In modern organizations we have systematically relegated the body to a low status. We have classified employees who work with their hands as manual workers or blue-collar employees. We have acknowledged the superiority of the intellectual white collar employees with increasing sophistication in production technology. The result has been a disproportionate emphasis on the thinking mind and an utter neglect of the untapped potential of our bodies. As the emerging sciences of the twenty-first century point toward the inseparable connection between the intelligence inherent in the mind-body system as a whole, it is time that we turn our attention to the culture of the unused intelligence in our bodies.

THE SENSES: TAMING WILD HORSES

Katha Upanishad, one of India's classical works of wisdom, describes the nature of our senses through the metaphor of horses driving a chariot. Says the Upanishad:

> Know the body as the chariot itself.
> Know that reason is the charioteer:
> and the mind indeed is the reins.
> The horses, they say, are the senses;
> and their paths are the objects of sense.

The description continues, as we obtain a vivid picture of the discipline of personal mastery, which is compared to taming wild horses:

> He who has not right understanding and whose mind is
>   never steady is not the ruler of his life, like a bad driver
>   with wild horses.
> But he who has right understanding and whose mind is
>   ever steady is the ruler of his life, like a good driver with
>   well-trained horses.

All classical wisdom has placed emphasis on the discipline of the senses as an important step toward personal mastery. This discipline involves understanding the nature of the senses and acting on that understanding. The body consists of five basic sense organs that enable us to process the reality of our environment. We attempt to see, smell, hear, taste, and touch our world through our senses. Our sense organs reach out to the world of events and objects and gather data for our minds to work on. When the mind is unsteady, the information presented to it by the senses becomes distorted. A turbulent mind reflects a disfigured version of reality as the ruffled surface of a lake distorts the image of the sun. As all decisions based on false data turn out to be ineffective, all sense perceptions based on distortion of reality are bound to be misleading.

The following Sufi story gives us a clear understanding of how problem solving is affected when our minds are disturbed and we are not in our senses:

> *A man saw Mulla Nasrudin, who was rather agitated and was looking for some lost property on the ground.*
> *"What have you lost, Nasrudin?" he asked.*
> *"The key to my house," said Nasrudin.*
> *So the man bent down to help Nasrudin look for the key.*
> *After a period of fruitless searching the man asked:*
> *"Nasrudin, where exactly did you drop the key?"*
> *"In my own house," Nasrudin replied.*
> *"Then why are you looking for it here?"*
> *"Because there is light here and there is no light in my house."*

Even when we are in our senses, our grasp of reality through sense perception is limited in range. In the ordinary state of awareness our senses do not even respond to one millionth of the total sensory stimulus present in a small room. We cannot, for example, smell the world with as much intensity as a dog does. We do not have the sharpness of vision of an eagle, which allows it to spot its prey from miles away. We also cannot hear the ultrasonic universe of which a bat can make sense. In the course of its evolution, the human species has lost much of its senses. We look with our eyes but fail to see; we hear sounds but fail to listen; we touch yet we do not feel.

Personal mastery in the realm of sense-perception can be achieved when we begin to see reality with a settled mind. This means we need to suspend our inner turmoil, quiet the clamor of voices that goads us into immediate judgments, and clear the cobwebs of past conditioning before we look at reality afresh.

One sure test of clarity of sense-perception is our ability to look into the smallest detail of sensory data that eludes the attention of many. Robert Greenleaf, former director of management research at AT&T, talks eloquently about enhancing our sensory awareness and its implications for leadership, as follows:

> Most of us move about with very narrow perception—sight, sound, smell, tactile—and we miss most of the grandeur that is in the minutest thing, the smallest experience. We also miss leadership opportunities. There is danger, however. Some people cannot take what they see when the doors of perception are open too wide, and they had better test their tolerance for awareness gradually. A qualification for leadership is that one can tolerate a sustained wide span of awareness so that one better "sees it as it is."
>
> ... ROBERT K. GREENLEAF, *Servant Leadership: A Journey into the Nature of Legitimate Power and Greatness*, 1977

Leadership requires a quality that is often called *common sense*. We cannot quite define what common sense is, yet we "sense" it when we see it. Common sense comes from a freshness of perspective. Common sense demands the childlike innocence of looking at reality without the conditioning of our senses. Those with common sense not only ask the correct questions but also question the very premise from which their questions come. Edward Deming, the pioneer of the total quality movement in industrial organizations worldwide, revolutionized management thinking through sheer common sense. Deming had no qualification in engineering or manufacturing. He was a statistician. Therefore he could look with a freshness of insight into the processes involved in manufacturing. He had still retained the common sense that most manufacturers lose as a result of extreme conditioning and specialization. Albert Einstein, who retained a child's innocence and inquisitiveness until the last day of his life, once said, "Small is the number of them that see with their own eyes and feel with their own hearts."

What are some of the ways we can discipline our senses to give us a more accurate interpretation of reality? One important discipline is to restrain ourselves from excessive sensory stimulation—watching too much television or indulging in gossip. All our sense organs habitually open outward. Content with collecting data from the external world, they remain closed to the depths to which they can inform us when they are turned inward. For example, sometimes when we are reflecting deeply on a subject, we tend to close our eyes. This is our instinctive way of drawing our sense of vision inward. The *Bhagavad Gita*, like all great scriptures of the world, describes the virtue of sense-discipline as the source of wisdom and mastery: "When a man can, like a tortoise that withdraws all its limbs, totally withdraw his senses from their objects, then he is a man of steady wisdom" (Chapter 2, verse 58).

Through our senses we receive two kinds of impressions. One kind of impression is the impression of the world around us. The other kind is the inner impression of what we feel about this world. Our reality is a combined creation of these two kinds of impressions. When our senses are open only to outside realities, they do not have a chance to pay attention to our inner reality. We have sight but fail to develop insight. We are content to eat junk food because it looks good, but we do not see the internal damage it does to us. We work in two jobs for the obvious monetary reward, but we do not respond with sensitivity to the resultant stress in our personal lives. By only half-seeing, we miss out on the essential unity of our reality—the unity of our becoming with our being.

Great leaders have an unfailing grasp of the nature of reality. This comes from a unique quality with which we often lose touch. It is our sense of proportion. Buddha is perhaps one of those rare leaders who achieved a rare sense of proportion in his lifetime. He discovered the middle path between austerity and indulgence and consequently led the world. More often than not, our undisciplined senses lead us to extremes of judgments, opinions, and biases, and we lose touch with reality. Leaders lose their following when they lose their hold on reality. George Bush, at the crest of a popularity wave after the Gulf War, lost the U.S. presidential election because he had not sensed the economic reality of the country. Indira Gandhi, India's prime minister for two decades, suffered a disastrous loss in one general election because she failed to sense popular resentment of her policies.

THE MIND: INNER INSTRUMENT

Try this experiment. Close your eyes for 30 seconds and visualize the word *tree*. Observe any tree that comes on your mind's screen. Explore your mental picture to the finest detail. What do you see there? A fir, a maple, or a eucalyptus? A palm tree swaying in the breeze? Or you saw no tree at all? Did you see only the word *tree* written on your mental map? You probably saw the green leaves of the tree and branches spreading like arteries. You may have seen the trunk of the tree or some flowers. Now ask yourself this important question, "Did I visualize the roots of the tree when thinking of a tree?" Ninety-nine out of one hundred of you will say, "No." But then the roots, though invisible to you, do exist. Don't they? The roots are in fact the most important component of a tree. Yet why does our mind miss such an important portion of the tree while visualizing it?

I have been asking the same question of people around the world from different cultures and different countries. Why don't we visualize the roots of a tree? I receive more or less the same answer, "Because we normally don't get to see the roots." What does this tell us? It tells us two things. First, our thought, which in the Western world is generally considered synonymous with *mind*, becomes conditioned by our sense-based data of reality. Second, our thought can process reality only by dividing the indivisible. Simply speaking, our thought is incapable of seeing the entire picture. Thought sees everything in fragments, and it cannot therefore comprehend the essential unity in nature.

In corporations people are paid to think of problems. But how many of us realize that sometimes our thinking itself is a problem? A thinking mind often lapses into rigid patterns. A thinking mind clings to definitions and dogmas. In his book *Future Edge* (1992), Joel Arthur Barker gives us an interesting list of quotations from well-known experts from the past who attempted to predict the future. Though their predictions may seem amusing in the present context, the following words will reveal the plight of thinking minds trapped in dogma and myopic vision:

> Flight by machines heavier than air is unpractical and insignificant, if not utterly impossible.
> ... SIMON NEWCOMB, an astronomer of some note, 1902

> It is an idle dream to imagine that ... automobiles will take the place of railways in the long distance movement ... of passengers.
> ... AMERICAN ROAD CONGRESS, 1913

> There is no likelihood man can ever tap the power of the atom.
> ... ROBERT MILLIKAN, Nobel Prize winner in physics, 1920

> Who the hell wants to hear actors talk?
> ... HARRY WARNER,
> Warner Brothers Pictures, 1927

> There is no reason for any individual to have a computer in their home.
> ... KEN OLSEN, president of Digital Equipment Corporation, 1977

Modern organizations thrive on extreme forms of specialization in products, services, and human power. This has given birth to the era of specialists. Specialists, whether engineers, doctors, computer analysts, or stock market wizards, use only a small part of their mental capacity. Any specialization involves taking the energy of thought to a certain groove or pattern. Thus thought becomes conditioned into patterns of energy and information. This results in narrowing the activities of the brain, which over time becomes limited in capacity, and its energy becomes less and less.

One amusing definition of a specialist is that he or she is a person who knows more and more about less and less. The specialist is conditioned to see the world from the perspective of instrumental knowledge. His vision is like that of the person with a hammer who sees the world as a nail. When he can't solve problems with a small hammer, he looks for a bigger hammer rather than a different instrument. Many specialists fail to solve problems they cause because their thinking becomes frozen and paralyzed in a given context. When a plan in an organization fails because of too much planning, which stifles action, the planning department hardly notices it. Instead, it indulges in even more rigorous planning without consulting the implementors—the managers in the field who may be able to pinpoint the flaws in the planning system. As Albert Einstein said, "The significant problems we face cannot be solved at the same level of thinking we were at when we created them."

Most of the problem-solving activities in our corporations involve the use of the left hemisphere of the brain. The cerebral cortex of the brain is divided into two hemispheres, joined by a bundle of interconnecting fibers called the *corpus callosum*. The left half of the brain is predominantly involved with analytical, logical, verbal, and quantitative functions. Its mode of operation is linear and sequential. The right half of the brain is intuitive, nonverbal, and holistic in its functions. Its mode of operation is relational. Thus the two halves of the brain display two modes of consciousness: the left half analyzes and recognizes the parts, the right half synthesizes and understands the whole picture. In our organizations and learning centers, the balance has in recent years shifted disproportionately to the left hemisphere of the brain with emphasis on verbal and logical modes of thinking. As a result, the right-brained functions of perceiving the whole system and seeing a problem in its context have been neglected.

The crisis of leadership in today's organizations can be ascribed to a crisis of thought. Peter Senge in his pioneering book, *The Fifth Discipline: The Art and Practice of Learning Organization*, articulates an important dimension of this crisis in his emphasis on systems thinking. Systems thinking, according to Senge, is a discipline for seeing wholes by describing and understanding the forces and relationships that shape the behavior of systems. One law of complex systems that Senge discusses is that the harder you push, the harder the system pushes you back. For example, when a product begins to lose market share, the normal pattern of thinking is to market it more aggressively. To do so, organizations spend more money on advertising or lower the price. In either case, the organization takes away resources from other parts of the organization, such as research and development and quality control. As a result, the quality of the product declines. In the long run the organization loses even more customers, and its market share declines further. Systems thinking involves both the left and the right sides of the brain—a grasp of the parts of a system and of the totality of the system. Our anxiety about unmanageably complex systems is reduced as we begin to understand the nature of relations between the various components of the system.

Systems thinking helps us to describe and continually clarify the nature of systems and patterns that emerge as we negotiate organizational reality. Yet systems thinking can have only a limited range of applicability, because thought itself is a system the dimensions of which are limited by the thinker. How can we expect a limited system such as thought to make sense of the unlimited data presented by reality?

If we begin to apply systems thinking to understand the nature of a flower, we will surely come up with a botanist's view of the flower, which is an organization of petals and sepals. A physicist is likely to see the flower as an arrangement of atoms and molecules. A chemist might give us an account of the flower's chemical composition. A poet describes the flower by putting together a set of beautiful words. Each of these views involves systems thinking. But the absolute reality of a single flower is so vast and infinite that all systems put together cannot comprehend even a portion of it. William Blake, the English poet, said: "If the doors of perception were cleansed everything would appear to man as it is, infinite."

By its very nature, thought itself is a fragmented system. Thought expresses itself in a systematic verbal structure or a language that has a logic and a limitation of its own. Whereas someone in Great Britain has one word to describe frozen water (*ice*), the Eskimos have at least six words to describe various states of ice. When a person in Great Britain thinks of ice, her reality is much less complex than when an Eskimo thinks of ice. Personal mastery consists as much in systems thinking as in realizing the inherent limitation of thought as a system. Sometimes we can solve complex problems by simply experiencing the problem and not by thinking about it. In a lighter vein we may say that if a centipede were to think about the system involved in moving its one hundred feet, the poor creature would be too confused to be able to walk. Neurophysiologists have confirmed to us that the body-mind is a collection of one hundred billion nerve cells. Yet we often think and act as one being. What is the mechanism that unites all our thoughts into one awareness? What is that awareness that makes our infinite impulses act in harmony within one organism?

Personal mastery comes from the lived experience of the fact that we are finite and infinite at the same time. We are finite to the extent we think we are so. But the essential reality of our being is that it is infinite. That we can see stars many light years away and that our bodies respond to the various rhythms of our cosmos are testimonies of our infinite nature. In the Western world, the notion of our being has been determined by our ability to think. Descartes said, "I think, therefore I am" (*Le Discours de la Méthode*, 1637). Western civilization interpreted this to mean that our essential being is defined by the action of thinking. Eastern civilizations, however, were not willing to concede their being to thinking alone. They reversed the theory of Descartes and said, "I am, therefore I think." It was a way of saying that our being precedes our thinking. The East did not consider thought as a limitation on our awareness as human beings. They went beyond the structure of thought in search of a deeper reality. It was from the foundation of this awareness that Indian masters challenged their disciplines to free the mind from the prison of thoughts.

The mind has been described in classical Indian wisdom as *antah karan*, the inner instrument. The instrumentality of the mind has not been confined to thoughts alone. In most Eastern civilizations, *mind* and *thought* are not synonymous. In these civilizations culture of the mind included the culture of both intellect and emotion. The Upanishads, for example, do not make a distinction between body and mind. The *rishis*, the masters in ancient India who gave us the wisdom of the Upanishads, did not experience the body and the mind as separate entities but as one continuum of consciousness. They used the term *monomaya kosha*, or mental body, to articulate their experience of mind-body connection.

The recent breakthroughs in mind-body medicine indicate to us that the ancient *rishis* of India were experientially aware of the quantum nature of our inner reality, which the modern sciences are beginning to acknowledge. The *rishis* clearly saw that the body was only a local expression of a universal field of conscious energy. They also understood that the mind was but a wave of information and energy in the huge ocean of universal consciousness. Body-mind was therefore not discrete but merely a gross and a subtle expression of the same universal consciousness. Scientists today are beginning to talk about thoughts in terms of thought fields. It is now known that when we believe we are hungry, our gut produces the same chemicals as our brain produces when it thinks of hunger. Studies also have shown that our gut and our brain biochemically express the notion of hunger at the same instant without any time lag between these expressions. That is, our brain thinks of hunger at precisely the same moment as our gut feels the hunger. This proves that mere awareness of hunger activates the mind-body field, which responds with a simultaneous reaction.

This new discovery has a profound implication for personal mastery and leadership. We can now begin to grasp the phenomenon of leadership as a field of awareness rather than a personality trait or mental attribute. We also can understand personal mastery as a play of consciousness that stretches beyond the frontiers of body-mind framework and the limited boundary of conscious thought. Scientists have arrived at the notion of the mind-body field by asking, "What is the nature of the objective reality?" The sages, however, have long discovered the same field by asking, "What is the nature of the self?" Sri Aurobindo, a modern sage of India, expresses this truth as an experiential reality of the self: "Know therefore thy body to be a knot in matter, thy mind to be a whirl in universal Mind and thy life to be an eddy of life that is forever." Albert Einstein expressed nearly the same truth when he reflected on the death of a close friend: "This death signifies nothing. For us, believing physicists, the distinction between past, present and future is only an illusion, even if a stubborn one."

How does one cultivate the mind to achieve personal mastery? The first step toward mind cultivation is to understand the nature of the mind. The ancient wisdom of India describes the human mind as a restless monkey. This monkey, the story goes on to say, in addition to being restless is intoxicated and is bitten by a scorpion. To add to its plight, the monkey is possessed by a demon. This description serves as a vivid metaphor of the mind as we see it in our day-to-day work.

Let us now understand the truths implied in the metaphors. The monkey-mind stands as a startling symbol of what may be called "a busy mind," which forever chatters and jumps from one thought to another. It is a mind with a short attention span, a mind that finds it difficult to concentrate on anything for too long. Intoxication, or a state of drunkenness, symbolizes excessive desire. A mind possessed by desire is in a high state of psychological arousal, which does not enable the mind to process data objectively. The *Bhagavad Gita* describes this state of mind in delightful poetry. "As a flame is covered by smoke, a mirror by dust and the foetus by the womb, so is knowledge covered by desire" (Chapter 3, Verse 38). To continue with the metaphor of the monkey-mind, the bite of a scorpion symbolizes the pangs of jealousy. The ordinary mind suffers through comparison. Jealousy does not end with sibling rivalry. It continues into our adult lives in many unrecognized forms. One of the negative aspects of competition within a corporation is this aspect of jealousy. Finally, the monkey-mind is possessed by a demon, which is a symbol of ego. When we are seized by a disproportionate ego, we lose our sense of proportion. When we don't have a sense of proportion, we lose our grasp on reality.

The classical psychology of India identifies four states of the mind. The first state is when the mind is agitated (*kshipta*). In this state the mind is in emotional turmoil and cannot function to its fullest extent. For example, when we are angry or hurt it becomes difficult for us to even answer a telephone call. The second state of the mind is when the mind is scattered (*vikshipta*). In this state the mind is fragmented in different directions as when we are trying to read a report, drink a cup of tea, and answer a telephone call at the same time. Needless to say, the mind cannot function with full efficiency in this state. The third state of the mind is the state of one-pointedness (*ekagra*). In this state the energy of the mind begins to focus on a single object or idea. When we love something we are doing, the mind is automatically one-pointed. However, through constant practice we can discipline the mind to be concentrated on anything we chose. A concentrated mind is much more effective than an agitated or a scattered mind.

The ancient seers did not stop at a concentrated mind. They explored further and arrived at a state in which the instrument called the mind dissolved into pure awareness (*niruddha*). This is a state of transcendence in which one begins to have an intuitive grasp of reality. We all experience this state sometime or another when solutions to difficult problems with which we are struggling simply "pop up" all of a sudden. A large amount of problem solving in our work-life happens when our conscious mind is allowed to rest completely. When the limited energy of conscious thinking accesses the unlimited energy of pure awareness, our minds work with greater effectiveness.

After we have observed the four states of the mind, we can begin to master the process of directing the mind toward greater perfection. We can do this at the following two levels—culture of emotions and culture of intellect. Although modern organizations and educational institutions place considerable importance to training the intellect, culturing the emotions has been completely neglected. We know, however, that our minds cannot function optimally unless we are emotionally balanced. As great leaders in history have often testified, emotion rather than intellect plays the primary role in decision making. Mahatma Gandhi knew, as he put it, that ultimately one is guided not by the intellect but by the heart. The heart accepts a conclusion for which the intellect subsequently finds reasoning. Argument follows conviction. Man often finds reason, Gandhi said, in support of whatever he does or wants to do.

Bertrand Russell echoed this truth when he said: "Even more important than knowledge is the life of emotion."

Tibetan Buddhist psychology describes five basic impure emotions that make the mind restless. They are as follows:

1. Anger (*khong-khro*)
2. Arrogance (*nga-rgyal*)
3. Indecision (*the-tshoms*)
4. Opinionatedness (*ita-ba*)
5. Cupidity attachment (*'dod-chags*)

Anger occurs when the mind becomes vindictive toward sentient beings and toward the source of one's frustrations. Arrogance is an inflated state of mind in which one is obsessed with one's superiority. Indecision is a state in which the mind is split in search for truth and is unable to establish a link between an action and its result. Opinionatedness is the mind's stubborn attachment to an opinion or dogma that is often misleading. Cupidity attachment is the mind's obsession with a pleasurable external or internal object.

All these impurities of the mind occur as a result of lack of emotional culture. To be able to come to grips with the unstable nature of the mind one needs to set aside moments of silence and solitude in one's daily life during which the mind begins to be aware of its inherent limitations. If we cultivate the habit of observing our emotions when they arise and take note of them, we will automatically find the impetus to change our negative emotions. The Sufis call this discipline, *zikr*, self-remembrance. A Sufi mystic, Jelaluddin Rumi, described *zikr* as an act of discrimination and as a discipline of delayed gratification, as follows (Barks, 1995):

> Don't try to control a wild horse by grabbing its leg.
> Take hold of the neck. Use a bridle. Be sensible.
> Then ride! There is a need for self-denial.

The benefit of self-remembrance is a state of mind Tibetan Buddhists call equanimity (*btang-snyoms*), as follows:

> What is equanimity? It is a mind that abides in a state of non-attachment, non-hatred, and non-deludedness coupled with assiduousness. It is quite dissimilar to a state that gives rise to emotional instability. It is a state where mind remains what it is— a state of being calm and a spontaneous presence of mind. Its function is not to provide occasions for emotional instability.
>
> . . . HEBERT GUENTHER AND LESLIE KAWAMURA (translators), *Mind in Buddhist Psychology*, 1975

Equanimity gives the mind purity of perception, clarity of vision, and effective decision-making capacity.

TOWARD AN INTEGRAL PERSON: THE LEADERSHIP PROFILE

Personal mastery is the ability to differentiate what we desire and what is desirable for us. This discipline not only enables us to make an intellectual distinction between the two but also empowers us to act on that distinction. All great leaders, all stable organizations, and all enduring civilizations have made this crucial choice in the course of their development.

Desire, like fire, is a source of natural energy and power. Just as it is possible to either harness the energy of fire for productive purposes or be burned by it, we may either be consumed by desire or harness it for the purpose of what is desirable.

Recall, for example, your last visit to the grocery store. As you walk through the store your eyes encounter a whole range of goods and foodstuffs jostling for your attention. Each of these products is packaged to arrest your attention and arouse your desire. If you were to follow your desire without discrimination, you would end up buying more things than you actually needed. Chances are, you would also pick up a great quantity of junk food, which would do your health no good. However, if you were a wise buyer, you would pick up only those things you really needed in exact proportion to your need for them. This may seem an easy job. But as all of us know, most of us end up buying more things than we need.

My father once told me an interesting story about a man who would go to the grocery store with a strange kind of shopping list. This list contained a large number of items that he was determined not to buy. This enabled him to keep his desire to buy on a leash. This is an amusing but an useful lesson to learn. That which we desire is often present before us in a tangible form. That which is desirable may not present itself immediately before our senses. The relatively obscure nature of the desirable makes it less alluring than a pressing desire.

Most of us who aspire to be leaders are quick to imitate the visible features of our idols' personalities—their lifestyles, the way they dress, how they talk. We forget that true leaders themselves have abandoned pursuit of trivial desires in search of the desirable. They have followed an ideal or a particular vision that is nothing but the essence of their lives reduced to its essential purpose. Leadership is the process of refining our perception of what we aspire in the ultimate sense. Martin Luther King could articulate his desirable goal of a nonracial America in his spellbinding words: "I have a dream." For Gandhi the ultimate goal was a state of self-perfection: "My life is my message." For President Gorbachev the vision was crystallized in a single expression: "*perestroika.*"

Although desires lead us to success, our quest of the desirable pushes us toward constant perfection. Whereas success comes from our motivation to achieve something, perfection goes beyond tangible motivation to the intangible realm of inspiration. The quest for perfection begins when the reference point for motivation has moved from the world outside to the self within. At this point, the creative tension that separates us from our goals has become part of our evolutionary urge. Our goals then integrate the stuff of our very being. We live the goal, we become the vision, and we realize the dream. While followers idealize the real, leaders realize the ideal. Toyota, the world's foremost automobile company, institutionalized the expression *kaizen* as its corporate mission. In Japanese, *kaizen* means continuous improvement. *Kaizen* extends the ethic of success to a higher point, the ethic of perfection. By not letting success diminish its quest for perfection, the leadership of Toyota has made a clear distinction between what is desired and what is desirable.

Organizations often recruit "balanced personalities" through aptitude and skills tests to manage resources. They look for specific personality types who they hope can deliver desired results for the organization. Although balanced personalities tend to perform and behave in a predictable manner, their balance often degenerates into static masks of conformism and conventional approaches to problem solving. Organizations are not static structures that can make do with balance alone. The essential dynamism of organizations calls for equilibrium, which is a higher order of stability than balance. Equilibrium is balance in motion; it requires the dynamism of a trapeze artist or a master gymnast. Equilibrium calls for creative responses to the demands of the moment.

Leadership is not an outcome of a balanced personality but the evolution of an integral person. Etymologically, the word *personality* comes from *persona*, which means a *mask*. In the usual sense this is what we understand by personality. It is a set of conventional social masks and an assortment of occupational skills that we use as a yardstick to measure a person's worth. But leaders wearing masks cannot inspire themselves or others. The true leadership profile is that of an integral person. Integral persons are those who integrate the energy of their entire being with their visions. Integral persons perform not out of a sense of contractual obligation but to realize their full potential. Integral performance does not require sanction of power from the higher-ups; it is self-empowering. Leadership comes naturally to integral persons for they serve with love. They outshine with their power of love those whose only motivation is love of power.

Michael Chalmers, studying for a master's degree in business administration, in class one day handed me a piece of paper on which he had printed a quotation by Warren Buffet, founder and president of Berkshire Hathaway. It came as a striking reminder to me how corporate leaders still value integrity in an age in which commitment and loyalty had become old-fashioned. Buffet points out that in looking for people to hire, you look for three qualities: integrity, intelligence, and energy. And if they don't have the first, the other two will kill you. You think about it, it's true. If you hire somebody without the first, you really want them dumb and lazy.

Personal mastery is a journey toward a destination we may call an *integral being*. Integral beings experience a life of oneness with themselves and their universe. They act from the wholeness of this experience. There is a harmony and a unique synchronicity between their beliefs and their actions. Their bodies, minds, and senses orchestrate themselves to the effortless rhythms of the universe. An integral person begins to experience spiritual affinity with the natural order of the universe; her inner nature becomes one with outer Nature. Her life becomes one song—a universe— of thought feeling and action. *Integrity* is another name for this one song. Integrity is a spontaneous expression of consciousness and not a conditioned behavior. In this consciousness our many aspirations are seen in their unity, we return to this unity at the end of our life's journey. True leadership, as we shall see in the next chapter, is an adventure of this consciousness.

2

Leadership and Consciousness

THE NATURE OF CONSCIOUSNESS

The following story will tell you a great deal about the nature of human consciousness. The hero of the story is Alexander, the great Macedonian emperor.

Alexander was camping on the border of the Indian subcontinent. He had marched triumphantly over half the world conquering and subjugating one kingdom after another in fierce battles. In a sense he was like the chief executive officer of a multinational corporation battling local competitors and grabbing market-share. In some places he struck strategic alliances with local chieftains and held control. In other countries he confronted his adversaries and raided their territories. On the threshold of his passage to India however, Alexander encountered a strange man. This man, dressed in a loincloth, would meditate for hours in a secluded place near Alexander's camp. For several days Alexander saw this sage seated in a lotus posture with eyes peering to the horizon. To Alexander this sage seemed like a lazy man, a recluse who had dropped out of life's race. This great warrior, unable to contain his curiosity one day, walked toward the sage and asked, "Don't you have anything to do besides sitting and dreaming."

The sage sat there unmoved.

"I see you every morning, evening, and afternoon in the same place and you have not moved an inch. You must be a terrible fellow!"

The sage did not speak a word.

Exasperated, Alexander asked, "Tell me what is your goal in life?"

Now, the sage smiled a little and said, "Great warrior, you must first tell me about your goal in life before I tell you mine."

Outraged, but still maintaining his calm, Alexander thundered, "Don't you know I am Alexander and I am out to conquer the world?"

The sage asked again, "What do you want to do after you've conquered the world?"

"Well," said Alexander, his lips curling in disdain, "I would then possess all the gold and all elephants and horses."

"And then," the sage prodded on.

"Then I would have all the men as my slaves."

"Then."

"Then I would have all the women to serve me."

"And then."

"Then I would sit on my throne, relax, and enjoy."

This time the sage looked straight into Alexander's eyes and said, "Sir, that is precisely what I am doing right now. Why are you bothering me? Please leave me alone and go ahead with your conquests."

Both Alexander and the sage are leaders who envision their world in the light of their own consciousness. Alexander seeks fulfillment in the conquest of the outward world of form and phenomenon. The sage searches for peace in the inner domain of subjective experiences.

Alexander's consciousness experiences the world as a battlefield, whereas the sage's consciousness experiences the same world as the field of self-realization. Alexander thinks, "How much more do I need to be happy?" while the sage ponders, "How much less can I have and still be happy?" Human motivation is a constant oscillation between two unasked questions that ring in our consciousness: "How much more do I need to be happy?" and "How much less can I have and still be happy?" The sage and Alexander live within all of us. They represent two fundamental states of human consciousness.

The questions that come to mind are: What then is the nature of consciousness? How can we grasp the notion of consciousness? Is consciousness synonymous with the process of our thinking? Is consciousness a state of feeling? Does it have an objective reality?

Let us look at the following attributes of consciousness:

1. Consciousness is universal. It is a primary state of our *being*. However, the process of *becoming conscious* differs from one person to another. To put it another way, consciousness is pure potentiality whereas becoming conscious is the process of actualizing this potentiality. A seed has the unrealized potential of a tree; the tree is hidden in the very being of the seed. This being is realized when the seed becomes a tree.

2. Consciousness is a qualitative aspect of life. It cannot be defined in precise terms. It can be experienced, however. Our consciousness of water comes from the qualitative aspect of *wetness*. No amount of chemical analysis of water can reveal to us the quality of wetness of water. We simply have to experience it.

3. Consciousness is the meeting point of the subjective and the objective. When mind meets matter, when thought perceives an object, consciousness is the outcome. The consciousness of sweetness of sugar comes from the relation between our subjective sense of taste and the objective property of the sugar molecule.

4. Consciousness is therefore a quality of relationship. This relationship is not static but dynamic and living. It differs from person to person and changes from one experience to another in the same person. We may have an exchange of angry words with a colleague in the morning but may be conscious of our anger only later in the evening when we have an occasion to relate to our experience.

5. There can be various states of consciousness, but these different states do not alter the fundamental nature of consciousness. The changing states of consciousness can be compared with the three different states of water as liquid, ice, and vapor. In each of these states the two ingredients of water, that is, hydrogen and oxygen, do not change in their fundamental composition. If you were to examine different samples of ice and

steam under a powerful microscope, the atoms of oxygen or hydrogen would look the same in both the samples. Yet ice does look different from steam to the naked eye. Extending this analogy to the nature of consciousness, we may say that it is not consciousness that changes, but it is our way of becoming conscious that changes from one human being to another.

6. Consciousness is therefore an integral, unchanging entity characterized by the qualities of wholeness and nondivisibility. As it is commonly misunderstood, consciousness is not a mechanical process generated by interaction within the human brain. As a matter of fact, scientists have located specific centers for thought and feeling within the human brain, but the seat of human consciousness has eluded their grasp. Thought can be analyzed and located in a specific place, but consciousness escapes such identification. In the structure of the human brain there are about ten billion nerve cells called *neurons*, which are interlined by a massive network of a thousand billion synapses. To stir a single thought in the maze of neurons and synapses, the brain has to activate countless biochemical reactions. All these require flawless programming and execution. It is our consciousness that performs such a complex task in the wink of an eye.

7. If consciousness cannot be objectively defined or identified, how can we then understand the nature of consciousness? Many modern physicists agree that the basic component of our physical universe is not matter but consciousness. Yet scientists are unable to provide us with a structure of consciousness. The unresolved enigma of consciousness is unique because, as a scientist told me, "consciousness itself is the only tool we have to examine consciousness." Thus the only way to search for consciousness is the self-referral process. That is, the self by referring back to itself establishes its own identity. Any search for consciousness in outward reality will be as futile as the eye's trying to look at itself. We are so intimate with our consciousness that we need only know ourselves to know consciousness. Consciousness is indeed a remarkable riddle of existence—that for which we are looking is indeed that which is looking.

THE EVOLUTION OF CONSCIOUSNESS

In the ancient sacred literature of India, known as the Upanishads, human life is viewed as an adventure of consciousness. The Upanishads personify the forces of nature such as fire, water, earth, and sky as living entities. The earth we walk on everyday is not inert matter as we tend to think it is. The earth is conscious! Our ancient seers as well as the most modern quantum physicist will testify to this.

Fritjof Capra, the eminent physicist, describes in his book *The Web of Life* the Gaia theory, which offers an alternative vision of our earth as a living system instead of seeing it as a dead planet consisting of inanimate rocks and oceans. Enunciated by James Lovelock, the Gaia hypothesis, which derives its name from the Greek goddess of the Earth, demonstrates that life on earth functions in a systemic way. This hypothesis states that life does not adapt to a passive environment; life actually makes and forms and changes the environment (Capra, 1996).

We must remember that all forms of life, including human life, have evolved from this very earth. The seed must open up to the intelligence inherent in the soil before it can become a plant or a flower. If this land mass, which we call our earth, were not conscious it would not be able to create a profusion of shapes and forms. There would not be such a delicate balance in our ecosystem or such a brilliantly programmed harmony between the million cells in our body. There would not be the wonderful symmetry in the two wings of a butterfly or the colorful camouflage of a chameleon.

The very process of human development is an unfoldment of the consciousness that permeates through all life forms on this earth. Interestingly, the word *development* has the same root as the word *envelope*. Development simply means *de-enveloping* or opening up the scripts of our lives. Our mind-body-senses structure is like an envelope that acts as a cover for our consciousness. This consciousness is the beginning of our lives and the end of it. To be in touch with this consciousness is the purpose of our work and life.

Human life and human mind have evolved in the stream of consciousness. In the course of human evolution, there was a time when the intellect of human beings had not fully developed. At that point of time, the consciousness of a human being functioned primarily at the level of instinct. Instinct served as a precise and scientific instrument for negotiating the problems of life. Even among tribal societies today, all over the world, we see the unerring power of the instinct. There are tribal people living in India today who can predict the onset of rains simply by sniffing the air! Aboriginal tribes in Australia can sense the right direction even in the middle of a storm. At the instinctual level, human consciousness functions primarily from biological memory, which is also the memory of Nature.

In the evolution of human consciousness, the human intellect arrived a little later than instinct. As civilizations grew out of jungles and forests into city states, the human mind began to function more out of psychological memory than biologic or natural memory. The mind of human beings was divorced from the mind of Nature. The intellect, which functioned primarily from psychological memory, slowly overshadowed the instinct, the origin of which was natural and biologic memory. With the intellect becoming the more reliable guide for thought and action, the instinctual intelligence of our consciousness was less and less in use.

CONSCIOUSNESS AS THE FIELD OF INTELLIGENCE

Consciousness is not static substance but a dynamic and intelligent entity. Consciousness is the basis of the interconnectedness of all form and phenomenon. Consciousness connects the diversity of existence into a unified expression. Imagine the human body, which is composed of several million cells—the heart cells, the brain cells, the stomach cells—each of which is a separate unit of life. Yet each of these cells functions in harmony with the other cells. When the brain cells "think" that the body is hungry, the stomach cells "feel" the same hunger. It is as if a wave of intelligence unites the brain cells and stomach cells into the experience of hunger. In other words, the brain cells have the consciousness of hunger just as the stomach cells do.

When we transfer this analogy to the realm of a complex and modern organization, we realize that a similar wave of intelligence connects one unit of the organization with another; otherwise the organization would not survive as one entity. The marketing unit must have an awareness of what the manufacturing unit is creating. The planning department must "think" on the same wavelength with the worker on the shop floor who has a "feel" for what the future holds for the company. The greater the flow of intelligence within the organization, the greater is the likelihood that the organization will function effectively. The emergence of cross-functional teams in the context of industrial organizations clearly indicates that corporations of the twenty-first century will try to harness the flow of intelligence within their constituents. In short, the corporations of tomorrow will try to become more and more conscious of themselves!

This brings us to a new understanding of organizational reality. We have begun to realize that organizations are not merely inert structures of units and departments but living fields of collective intelligence of the people who constitute the organization. This collective field of intelligence is what we may call *consciousness*. In this sense organizations are conscious entities through which intelligence flows. The goals and objectives of the organization give direction to this flow while the people working for the organization become conscious conduits through which this flow maintains its momentum. The organization serves as a matrix or a field on which structures and processes, machines and people and mechanisms mesh together to facilitate the play of creative energy.

The notion of the *field* as a metaphor for reality emerged in modern physics in the early nineteenth century. Michael Faraday and James Maxwell introduced the concept of force fields as an alternative to the idea of mechanical force described by Newton, which could be explained only with reference to material objects interacting with other. Unlike mechanical force, the notion of force fields extended the understanding of *force* from a purely material reality to another dimension. In a force field, the presence of the field was self-evident, and this could be investigated without reference to an object. Thus a field was constituted not by material objects but by a nonmaterial influence or a force such as a gravitational force or a magnetic force.

We shall take the example of a bar magnet and metal pins to illustrate the characteristics of a field force. We shall see that the magnetic field of the bar magnet is not limited by material boundaries. It is an invisible, open, and objectless field. This field is present everywhere in the vicinity of the magnet. One can experience this presence as a force by placing a pin anywhere in its zone of influence. Moreover, if several pins are scattered at random around the magnet, they will organize themselves into a distinct pattern according to the nature and distribution of the magnetic field.

If we were to try to imagine an organization as a field of intelligence, we would realize that the organization has apparently no material boundaries. The charismatic chief executive officer of General Electric, Jack Welch, evaluates his executives on how well they embody the corporate value of boundarylessness, among other traits. We can understand this notion of boundarylessness more vividly if we realize that the boundary of an organization is determined by its very last customer or stockholder. No organization can determine with precision the finishing line of its potential customer, on whom the organization's field force will exert an influence. Organizations are forever enhancing their capacity to influence the last customer.

If we turn our attention within the organization, we see that much like the patterned positioning of the pins, the roles and identities of the employees of the organization evolve in a certain pattern, which we describe as the *culture* of the organization. The members of the organization, unlike the pins, are not passive units. They are creative individuals who can consciously co-create the organizational culture. Each individual who imbibes a specific corporate culture acts like organizational DNA and becomes capable of preserving and transmitting this culture across space and time. This explains why multinational corporations can maintain a certain cultural identity even when they operate in different geopolitical settings.

To return to our understanding of consciousness as the field of intelligence, we will try to understand the evolution of quantum mechanics in the first half of the twentieth century. In the 1920s physicists led by Werner Heisenberg described our universe not as a collection of separate objects but as a web of relations between various parts of a unified field. Heisenberg's *matrix mechanics* was the first logical step toward what we understand as the quantum theory. The quantum physicists pondered over the behavior of subatomic phenomena and came to the conclusion that our material world is not a mechanical construct of separable objects. It is a relational matrix on which apparently separate objects are held together by a common ground of invisible energy.

Fritjof Capra in his book *Uncommon Wisdom* describes how physicists in the early 1920s used to be puzzled by the dual nature of subatomic particles they were examining with a microscope. These physicists were amazed how the same electrons would behave like "particles on Mondays and Wednesdays and waves on Tuesdays and Thursdays" (Capra, 1988). Werner Heisenberg attempted to unravel the mystery behind this phenomenon with his uncertainty principle. This principle, stated in simple language, meant that uncertainty in the behavior of the observed electron was caused by the observer-scientist who was influencing the behavior of the electron in certain ways on Mondays and Wednesdays and in certain other ways on Tuesdays and Thursdays. Heisenberg pointed toward an integral connection between the observer, the thing observed, and the process of observation.

In reality, quantum physicists asserted, all three were inseparable phenomenon. Albert Einstein, who along with Heisenberg and Niels Bohr established the quantum theory, explained how our theories determine what we intend to measure. Thus the world, which in 300-year-old Cartesian logic is seen as a mechanical structure of separate and unrelated objects, was perceived by quantum scientists as a deep-seated illusion of our minds. Heisenberg rightly pointed out that the Cartesian partition has penetrated deeply into the human mind during the three centuries since Descartes and that it will take a long time for it to be replaced with a completely different attitude about the problem of reality.

The conception of quantum mechanics, in which the ever-changing world of form and phenomenon is seen as temporary manifestations of an underlying field, is something that the mystics of the East realized thousands of years ago. The mystical revelations of Buddha, Krishna, and Lao-tzu were of the same stuff as the revolution of Einstein's quantum physics. Fritjof Capra, in *The Tao of Physics* described this eloquently, as follows:

> Subsequent to the emergence of the field concept physicists have attempted to unify the various fields into a single fundamental field which would incorporate all physical phenomena. Einstein, in particular, spent the last years of his life searching for such a unified field. The Brahma of the Hindus, like the Dharmakaya of the Buddhists and the Tao of the Taoists, can be seen, perhaps as the ultimate unified field from which springs not only the phenomena studied in physics, but all other phenomena as well.
>
> . . . FRITJOF CAPRA, *The Tao of Physics*, 1975

FOUR STATES OF SELF-CONSCIOUSNESS

The psychology of Vedanta and Buddhism tells us that mind and matter are merely two contrasting poles of pure consciousness. According to this psychology, both mind and matter emerge from a unitary consciousness. In the process of manifestation, the mind emerges as the subjective, invisible polarity of consciousness. On the other hand, matter assumes the objective, visible dimension of the same consciousness. Thus if matter is unconscious, its polar opposite, the mind, has the gift of consciousness.

Thus matter is nothing but mind made visible. The Upanishads clearly say, "Things are thoughts."

This is a very powerful experiential insight coming from our ancient psychologists. I believe that such an insight is not an empty speculation but has its basis in reality. If we were to trace the evolutionary history of the human mind from gross matter of mineral, plant, and animal world, we would realize how the mind has become increasingly subtle and sophisticated. The unique capacity of the human mind that distinguishes it from that of any other species is its ability to be conscious of itself. This self-conscious nature of the mind provides it with a stimulus for further evolution, which is to be completely conscious of itself. This means that the human mind has the potential to completely merge with its source—consciousness itself. The mystical experience of attaining to pure consciousness without an object has been described in religious literature as *nirvana*, *samadhi*, or *enlightenment*, all of which are synonymous with complete *self-realization*.

The classical psychology of India describes the following four states of human consciousness:

1. The waking state, or *jagrat*.
2. The dream state, or *swapna*.
3. The dreamless sleep state, or *sushupti*.
4. The state of pure consciousness, or *turiya*.

Jagrat is the ordinary waking and thinking state of consciousness. It is the state in which most of us spend our waking hours. In *jagrat* we comprehend the world through the structure of conscious thoughts. Our understanding of reality in this state is primarily sensory reality processed by our five sense organs. Because our sense-organs are limited in their ability to process all the reality in our environment, our waking state can give us only a fragmented view of things.

Swapna is the dream state of our consciousness. Although dreams may appear very unreal from the point of view of our waking state, they are nevertheless very real in the context of our dream bodies. We have to understand that dreams do not take place in an imaginary sphere outside ourselves. We experience the sensation of our dreams in our psychophysiologic structures in the form of cold sweat when we have nightmares. We also experience real movement of our limbs when we encounter a dream accident. In the dream state the subconscious experiences of our waking state are acted out in the language of dreams. The dream language is a metaphoric language that does not obey the logic of ordinary language. This language, however, is as real in its context as any other language—the only problem is that we seem to lack the skill to interpret it. Most tribal cultures have ways of interpreting dreams of different kinds. In modern times many scientists have found clues to their inventions and discoveries in the dream state. In the sphere of management, too, the possibility of exploring the dream state for insights into effective decision making has been researched by Dr. Francis Menezes of the House of Tatas, the largest industrial House of India.

Sushupti is the state of deep sleep. Ordinarily, we equate the state of deep sleep with a state of unconsciousness. Classical Indian psychology, however, considers *sushupti* a profound state of self-consciousness. Take the example of a person who says, "I had such deep and blissful sleep that I was not aware of anything." Two interpretations emerge from this statement. First, the person was not aware of anything that disturbed his sleep. Second, at the same time the person had the awareness or experience of a blissful state in which he slept soundly. Unless there existed an experiencer of the blissful state, how can the person remember it when he is awake. The Indian masters identified this experiencer as a state of consciousness they called the higher self or simply the Self (with a capital *S*).

Ramana Maharshi, the great Indian master, explained this dual state of awareness and ignorance in deep sleep as follows. The peaceful awareness is due to the absence of the torrent of thoughts in deep sleep, and the ignorance is due to the absence of objective and relative knowledge of the waking state. In *sush-upti*, consciousness is freed from the prison of thoughts, so the Self experiences a sense of freedom much like a bird that escapes its cage to the peace of a vast blue sky. As Ramana Maharshi says, "Deep sleep is nothing but the experience of pure being."

Turiya is a transcendental state of consciousness. It is not an exclusive state like the states of waking, dreaming, and sleeping but is an inclusive state that is present in the other three states. *Turiya* is pure consciousness, which forms the substratum of all other states of consciousness. In the words of Ramana Maharshi, "*Turiya* is another name for the Self. Aware of the waking, dream and sleep states, we remain unaware of our own Self. Nevertheless the Self is here and now, it is the only Reality." *Turiya* is the ground reality of consciousness. It is the field of awareness—the ultimate quest of all our knowledge and experience.

The foregoing states of Self-consciousness are not theories spun by philosophers. They are, in real terms, experiential states accessible to every human being. They are realized experiences of transformed consciousness of human beings like you and me. This transformation occurs at the level of the Self. As Gandhi once said, "I must first be the change I wish to bring about in my world."

THE LEADER AS THE HERO: THE TRANSFORMATION OF CONSCIOUSNESS

I was hearing Joseph Campbell, the man who dedicated his entire life to understanding myths, in a videotape titled *The Hero's Adventure*. Campbell said that all myths have to deal with transformation of consciousness. According to him, all mythologic heroes have undergone this process of self-transformation in trying to seek out something larger than life. The transformational journey of the hero, according to Campbell, consists of losing oneself and of giving oneself to another.

In the cold, calculating world of business the notion of heroism may appear rather out of place. Yet we cannot ignore the fact that all great entrepreneurial acts have been nothing short of heroic feats. Great corporate leaders such as Akio Morita in Japan, Lee Iacocca in the United States, and Jamsetji Tata in India have embraced challenges of life of heroic proportions. Their lives are woven around the stuff of corporate myths. Another example is Yotaro Kobayashi, chairman of Fuji Xerox and Japan's most prominent international industrialist. As a young man Kobayashi was greatly motivated by time spent in what he calls "the presence of greatness." Kobayashi's heroic model was none other than Joe Wilson, the man who built the xerography business. Kobayashi tells how he became imbued with the power of corporate heroism: "Only by meeting a person face to face—not once but several times—can you sense their qualities. . . . There are things you only feel. You ask yourself, How can I do this ?"

What then is the source of the hero's power? As a matter of fact, heroes transcend the limitations of the intellect to attain the power of Nature from which our minds separates us. The power of heroic leadership cannot be grasped with the intellect alone, it has to be felt. One is reminded again of Gandhi's words: "I know that ultimately one is guided not by the intellect but by the heart. The heart accepts a conclusion for which the intellect subsequently finds reasoning." Managerial leadership that aspires to heroism must sometimes suspend the calculations of the intellect and go by the convictions of the heart.

The advice that Campbell gives to the would-be-hero is: "Put yourself in a position where you evoke your higher nature." And how does one put oneself in touch with one's higher nature? By means of a transformational journey of the consciousness. The next question one would ask is: How does one undertake such a transformational journey? Campbell answers: "By the trials. A test or certain illuminating revelations. Trials and revelations that is what it is all about. Heroes go into regions where no one has gone before" (Campbell, 1968).

Consciousness is therefore the edge that separates the mediocre from the heroic. This consciousness is the gateway to our own mystery and the passport to our ultimate possibility. The Vedantic psychology tells us that the ultimate source of human consciousness is a center of bliss and absolute peace. The Sanskrit word for such a state is *ananda*. It is a state beyond conscious thought, a place of absolute stillness amid the wild turmoil of life. *Ananda* is not an other-worldly state. We all have experienced it at some time or another. Basketball players in championship form find the center of quietude from which all their actions flow flawlessly. So do the greatest musicians and the greatest painters. A leader who has had a revelation of this state of consciousness finds the secret of his peak performance.

We can see that heroism is a very human possibility. Why then do we have so few heroes in real life? Why can't we all aspire to be heroes? In fact, we all do! We project our quest for heroism onto our stars on the sports field and celluloid screens. Doing so saves us the trial that our heroes go through in the arena of action. Most of us therefore feel comfortable in being arm-chair heroes. The world is indeed full of people who have stopped responding to the intensities of their own selves and look for heroism in the world outside. When we begin, however, to realize that heroism is nothing but a heightened awareness of our Self we will probably begin to look within. Yotaro Kobayashi, at the age of 63, inspires young executives to undertake the heroic journey by clearing the cobwebs of mystery that envelop the corporate hero. He says that once young people can recognize their heroes as human, they can begin to find heroism in themselves.

THE MIDDLE PATH:
THE WAY OF RIGHT PERCEPTION

The gospel of Buddha emphasizes right livelihood as one of the secrets of a happy life. The leadership journey is essentially a search for right livelihood through right perception. What then is the secret of right livelihood and right perception? For this, we turn to *The Dialogues of Plato*, in which the great Greek master records the following dialogue between Socrates and Adeimantus on the reason for the deterioration of the quality of life:

> **Socrates:** There seem to be two causes of the deterioration of the arts.
>
> **Adeimantus:** What are they?
>
> **Socrates:** Wealth, I said, and poverty.
>
> **Adeimantus:** How do they act?
>
> **Socrates:** The process is as follows: When a potter becomes rich, will he, think you, any longer take the same pains with his art?
>
> **Adeimantus:** Certainly not.
>
> **Socrates:** He will grow more and more indolent and careless?
>
> **Adeimantus:** Very true.
>
> **Socrates:** And the result will be that he becomes a worse potter?
>
> **Adeimantus:** Yes; he greatly deteriorates.
>
> **Socrates:** But, on the other hand, if he has no money, and cannot provide himself with tools or instruments, he will not do equally well with himself, nor will he teach his sons or apprentices to work equally well.
>
> **Adeimantus:** Certainly not.
>
> **Socrates:** Then, under the influence, either of poverty or of wealth, workmen and their work are equally liable to degenerate?
>
> **Adeimantus:** This is evident.
>
> **Socrates:** Here, then, is a discovery of new evils, I said, against which the guardians will have to watch, or they will creep into the city unobserved.
>
> **Adeimantus:** What evils?
>
> **Socrates:** Wealth, I said, and poverty; the one is the parent of luxury and indolence and the other of meanness and viciousness, and both of discontent.
>
> . . . PLATO, *The Republic*, IV, 421-B

This dialogue puts us in touch with the way a great leader of men arrives on the middle path of right perception. Socrates' perceptive wisdom neither glorifies nor vilifies wealth or poverty. The Greek master takes our awareness beyond the objective world of poverty and wealth to the subjective world of wealth consciousness and poverty consciousness. He seems to suggest that a consciousness obsessed with the thoughts of either wealth or poverty is the source of discontent. The way out is to find the golden mean in the realm of consciousness whereby neither wealth nor poverty can affect our quality of life.

In a capitalistic society in which "the more, the merrier" is the guiding motto of life, the reasoning of Socrates may fall on deaf ears. But there is no denying the fact that the emerging realities of a "the more the merrier" way of life will tell us that Socrates is telling a stark truth. Examine the truth in the following statement: we become poor not because of what we do not have but because of what we desire but cannot have. We will realize that poverty is a mental state that is a function of our mental discontent. Poverty consciousness cannot be satiated with wealth alone unless the mental discontent is taken care of. The Greek fable of King Midas who would turn everything he touched into gold is a good example of this concept.

The wisdom of Socrates lies not in defining wealth or poverty in material terms but in his firm grasp of the inner world of human beings. Socrates is speculating not on our standard of living but on our quality of life. It is often said that our age is a quantitative age in which everything is measured in terms of numbers. Our standard of living is a numerical measure of our worth as human beings in terms of how much money we possess, how many cars we have, and so on. Quality of life deals not so much with external measures of life as it does with an internal sense of well-being. Another Greek master, Heraclitus, once said, "Man is the measure of all things." It is another way of saying that a sense of proportion exists in the inner constitution of a human being. A leader of men and women finds the Golden Mean of inner poise within the Self.

A leader strikes a harmonious relationship in her inner world. She achieves a measure of equilibrium between her active and contemplative life. She is not caught in the whirlpool of meetings and office politics all her waking hours. She sets aside time to have an appointment with herself in a quiet corner of her chamber for half an hour everyday. In the workplace, where most of us do not even have a chance to say hello to our inner selves, setting aside time for self-acquaintance helps restore the much needed harmony in our lives. All great leaders instinctively know this.

The notion of the middle path is an important life skill that a leader has to cultivate. In our workplaces, where frequent emotional transactions take place between leaders and co-workers, it is important for the leader to demonstrate emotional equanimity and balance in dealing with colleagues. When the follower perceives the slightest bias in the leader's emotional disposition toward a particular co-worker, the credibility of the leadership process suffers. Ordinary minds are easily swayed by likes and dislikes.

His Holiness the Dalai Lama, the spiritual leader of Tibet, tells us about a simple test to measure our emotional balance. He says that to equalize your feelings, begin by visualizing three people in front of you—a very close friend, an enemy, and a neutral person. Having visualized these three people, let your mind react naturally. You will find that your mind reacts in an unbalanced way. You find yourself attached to the friend and repelled by the enemy, and your attitude to the third person will be one of indifference.

Often in the workplace we find it difficult to make objective decisions about people because we are terribly attached to our first impressions of them. To cultivate a just and objective attitude to people at work, leaders have to culture their emotions in the light of truth and objectivity. This requires a tireless pursuit of the middle ground between attachment and animosity. The Dalai Lama sheds further light on this subject, as follows:

> This is not to suggest that we do not have friends and enemies. What we are concerned with here is to offset our drastic, imbalanced emotional reactions to others. This equanimity is very important; it is like first leveling the ground before cultivating it.
> . . . DALAI LAMA, *The Way of Freedom*, 1995

In life, as in work-life, we encounter many paradoxes. A paradox is a natural state in which two apparently contradictory processes happen simultaneously. To take a simple example, the more wholesome food we eat, the more nourished we are. The same wholesome food, however, taken even slightly more than necessary turns into toxins in the body. The way to negotiate this paradox is to take the middle path of dietary discipline and to know just how much food is too much. If we sharpen a saw, it can cut wood better. If, however, we sharpen the saw too much, the edge of the saw becomes too fragile to do its job. Farmers who grow crops know of a wonderful paradox of nature. They know that the more manure they use, the greater is the yield of crops. At the same time, however, they are aware that beyond a certain measure the greater use of manure does not yield a proportionately greater output of crops. In economics this phenomenon is known as the *law of diminishing returns*.

A leader develops an innate ability to negotiate paradoxes. He instinctively knows the exact point where the laws of nature reverse themselves. This knowledge comes to him because he follows the Middle Path, the way of right proportion. Right proportion is not necessarily an outcome of quantitative measurements or a statistical probability. Right proportion is the path of right perception that comes from the luminosity and clarity of consciousness. The leader is extremely alert and sensitive to the subtle laws of Nature, including human nature. She knows when loyalty turns into flattery and when genuine commitment degenerates into soulless compliance. All these she understands because her alert mind can read the silent language of Nature which is the language of paradoxes.

LEADERSHIP AND COSMOCENTRIC CONSCIOUSNESS

Talking about his transformational journey toward becoming a world leader Gandhi once said: "There comes a time when an individual becomes irresistible and his action becomes all-pervasive in its effect. This comes when he reduces himself to zero." Gandhi's words may appear awkward for leaders whose basis of power is centered on title, designation, qualifications, perks, paychecks, and a grand self-image. Yet when we examine Gandhi's statement with the objectivity of a scientist, we realize its validity.

First, let us understand what Gandhi means by the expression "reduces himself to zero." Ordinarily, the symbol *0* gives us an impression of nothingness. Yet we know that zero is a powerful entity in the world of mathematics. In real terms, zero may not appear to have tangible, material value. But we all know that it has positional value in the sense that it can "create" great value when placed after a number.

A zero can fundamentally alter the quantitative and qualitative value of any given number. Zero is indeed the domain of infinite potentiality. Any number divided by zero becomes infinity. A number multiplied by zero assumes the nonfinite quality of zero itself. Thus we can say that in qualitative terms, the symbol *0* has a touch of the infinite in it. In short *0* implies not only emptiness of matter but also the fullness of a nonmaterial presence. We may call this nonmaterial presence *intelligence*.

Isaac Asimov in a book titled *Words of Science* traces the etymologic history of *0* to India. According to Asimov, *0* traveled from India with Arabs to western Europe in the Middle Ages. The Arabs called that symbol *sifr*, which means *empty*. This *sifr* came to us in the English language as *cipher*, which means "to solve an arithmetical problem." From *cipher* we get the word *decipher*, which means "to find the meaning of something which is puzzling" (Asimov, 1959).

We come back to the puzzle and the mystery of the origin of *0*. In India, where this symbol was supposed to have originated, the zero is known as *shunnyo* or the *void*. The great Indian minds were not content with using zero as a symbol or a concept, they wanted to understand *0* as a real experience. Buddha's experience of *nirvana* was nothing but the qualitative experience of zero. The Buddhists call it *shunnyata*. This was Buddha's experience of the field of consciousness free of objects. In reality an object is something that objects or hinders the flow of consciousness. This unhindered flow of consciousness is the ground reality of all form and phenomenon. Therefore, *0* is a powerful metaphor for the reality of our existence. The zero is something of nothing. The zero is an existential void that none of us can avoid.

As we move from the philosophical to the experiential understanding of *0*, we know why Gandhi is urging us to reduce ourselves to zero. When we closely examine our self-concepts, we realize that all that we imagine we are revolves around the center of our ego. An egocentric person feels empowered by things and objects he can possess. In fact, he reduces even human beings to the status of objects he can manipulate. This object-centered self-identity is vulnerable and transitory, simply because the objects themselves are everchanging and perishable. If we identify ourselves with the money we earn, any decrease in our income torments us. If we identify ourselves with our children, we feel like empty nesters whenever our children leave us. The ego's identification with external objects and events is self-defeating in the long run. Progressive reduction of our material identification will enable us to develop our nonmaterial dimension.

This development of the nonmaterial dimension of our lives helps us to progress from egocentric personalities to what we may call *cosmocentric individuals*. Cosmocentricity places individuals in harmonious relation with the laws of Nature. If we look deeply into all the phenomena of Nature, we see cosmocentric consciousness at work. The little sunflower centers its entire attention on the sun and turns its face toward sunlight for sustenance. The huge earth spins precisely at the same speed on its axis day after day under some cosmic spell. An unerring intelligence connects our small lives to the vastness of our cosmos. This intelligence becomes accessible to us the moment we begin to read Nature's manuscript. The English poet William Blake gave us a glimpse of cosmocentric life in delightful poetry:

> To see a world in a grain of sand
> And a heaven in a wild flower,
> Hold infinity in the palm of your hand
> And eternity in an hour.
>
> . . . WILLIAM BLAKE,
> "Auguries of Innocence," c. 1805

Cosmocentric consciousness is our natural state. We simply need to allow it to happen to us. By freeing our lives and minds from time to time from the clutter of objects and our possessions we can flow into this state. When we deeply contemplate on ourselves it becomes clear to us that the same consciousness that orchestrates the movement of planets in our solar system also organizes the various movements within our body into a harmonious existence. Rabindranath Tagore, the great mystic poet, told us: "The same stream of life that runs through my veins night and day, runs through the world and dances in rhythmic measure."

Leaders are in touch with the creative rhythm of cosmic consciousness. Their spontaneity comes from an experience of oneness with their followers, through whom the same consciousness runs its course. The leader-follower relationship is one of unity of consciousness. The Sanskrit word for this is *ekatmanubhuti*. Leadership and followership cannot be differentiated in a state of *ekatmanubhuti*. They merge in the common ground of a unity of consciousness. Leaders lead from the heart. Their lives pulsate with the grand rhythms of the cosmos. Followers follow from the heart. They see in their leaders the manifestation of universal natural order. Describing this power, Emerson compared it to light and heat, and all Nature cooperates with it. "The reason why we feel one man's presence and do not feel another's," he said, "is as simple as gravity."

LEADERSHIP AS A STATE OF CONSCIOUSNESS

Lao-tzu, China's most influential sage and political ruler in the fifth century B.C., had astute insights into the process of effective leadership. For the Chinese master, leadership was not a competitive game but had a close kinship with the development of human consciousness. Lao-tzu spoke of four different levels of consciousness, which give rise to different kinds of leaders:

> There are four different levels of ruler. The highest is the one who leads without words, allowing the people to follow their own natures and live their own lives.
> The next highest is the ruler who uses virtue to transform the people and benevolence and righteousness to govern them.

The next is the ruler who controls his people with political teachings and scares them into submission through strict laws and punishments.

The worst kind of ruler uses all his powers to mislead his people with devious schemes.

In Lao-tzu's hierarchy of leadership, the best form of leadership is to be conscious of the leadership potential within the followers and to let them unleash this potential in a spontaneous way. According to him, when a great leader accomplishes this task with effortless ease, the followers say, "We did it ourselves." Lao-tzu was talking about the process of empowerment, which is often misunderstood in the context of corporate leadership.

Empowerment is not about giving power to the other in the physical sense of the term. It is about energizing and developing the source of power that the other already possesses. A staff member in research and development may not necessarily be empowered if given higher managerial responsibility in the organization. On the other hand, she may truly feel empowered if one of the products she designs is given recognition by the organization. Max DePree in a *Fortune* magazine interview said:

> Take a 33 year old man who assembles chairs. He's been doing it several years. He has a wife and two children. He knows what to do when the children have ear-aches, and how to get them through school. He probably serves on a volunteer board. And when he comes to work we give him a supervisor. He doesn't need one. His problem isn't to be supervised, it's to continue toward reaching his potential.
>
> . . . MAX DEPREE, *Fortune*, March 26, 1990

Empowering leadership is a conscious process of capacity building—recognizing capacity and developing it. Goethe described this process beautifully: "If you treat an individual as he is, he will remain as he is. But if you treat him as if he were what he ought to be and could be, he will become what he ought to be and could be."

It requires extraordinary ability to discover sparks within an individual and to allow this spark to become a fire of inspiration

for the pursuit of a goal. Leadership facilitates the conscious evolution of followers' capacity for action. It is also an evolution of
consciousness. Bill Gates, chief executive officer of Microsoft, is a
prime example of what a conscious leader is. About his leadership style he says:

> You don't just think about what a company does and try to do it
> faster. You want to empower somebody like a product manager
> to be able to digest more things. Why do you have meetings?
> Well, the top executive has more data than other people, so he has
> to have meetings to share his data. What if everybody had the
> same data and had a better way to look at it? Would you need as
> many meetings, as many levels of management? Maybe not.
>
> . . . BILL GATES, *Fortune*, March 26, 1990

Glancing through the leadership profiles of many eminent
men and women in the history of civilization, I have come to
realize that leadership is neither a science nor an art; it is a state
of consciousness. Conscious leadership follows three fundamental processes. The first of these is recognition of potential. The
second is empowerment of potential. And the last but not the
least is unfolding this potential through collective action. Recognition of potential requires an eagle's eye for details; empowerment of potential requires a lion's heart for sharing power; and
the capacity for collective action requires the perseverance of an
ant. The last quality can be developed only when the leader
understands the nature of work and the secret of transformational action. This is what we deal with in chapter 3.

3

Leadership and Work

THREE RULES OF WORK

Albert Einstein gave us three rules of work. They were as follows:

1. Out of clutter, find simplicity.
2. From discord, find harmony.
3. In the middle of difficulty lies opportunity.

The first rule implies recognition of a specific ideal toward which we wish to work. Gandhi worked for the simple ideal of nonviolence, and his life was dedicated to that single cause. Such was the power of that cause that it enabled one man to stand up against the then greatest empire on earth. The search for an ideal involves getting in touch with the deepest yearning of our nature. We need to understand what is it that we deeply care about. What is it that we want to give birth to through our work? Work that is not hitched to a guiding principle degenerates into a mundane chore and loses its meaning. Imagine the plight of Nelson Mandela spending decades in prison in South Africa. If his life had not been guided by the quest for freedom for himself and his countrymen and countrywomen, he would have been a nervous wreck after all those years of confinement.

Our day-to-day work-lives are cluttered with a thousand competing priorities. When we are mentally occupied with all these priorities, we become stressed to the limit, and our psychological energy is dissipated. When we have an ideal clearly etched in our consciousness, however, all our priorities tend to organize themselves in relation to that clear and simple ideal. An ideal is like a magnetic iron bar around which myriad iron filings organize spontaneously.

A successful corporate leader in India has an impressive plaque hung on the wall behind his worktable. Golden letters proclaiming the one ideal of his work-life shine out from the plaque. They read: *Success is not the aim of my work. Perfection is.*

How does this ideal serve this man's purpose in day-to-day life in which success is the only measure of development? The young leader replies cheerfully as follows:

> Many people ask me this question, but, as you will know, in real life, success comes along with failures. For every contract I succeed in getting, I fail in three. If success were my life's only ideal, failures would depress me terribly and that would affect my work-life. So, every time I fail in my work, I look at those words and tell myself: I've got to do better, for perfection is the only aim of my world.

A sound ideal this. The power of this ideal comes not only from a few simple words but also from the lived experiences of life. The greater the depth of our perception of our lives, the greater is the power of an ideal. At great depth, life simplifies itself into one or two basic laws or principles of existence. Henry David Thoreau (*Walden*, 1854), with his unerring insight into human nature once said: "Our life is frittered away by detail . . . Simplify, simplify."

Einstein's second rule is, from discord find harmony. This is an extension of the first rule. The first step toward search for harmony is to find coherence within one's own self in the context of work. This means that my head and my heart must be together in the work that I do. If they are not, my work is not an extension of my self. In other words, what I do is not what I love doing. There are published reports of the fact that a large number of people in the United States die of heart attacks on a specific day and at a specific time—Monday morning, nine o'clock. This is ample evidence of the many "living deaths" that we die every Monday morning when we reluctantly drag ourselves to work. That fatal event one Monday morning when a heart attack claims us is merely an extension of a series of nonevents in which we succumb to a heartless job.

The next step toward search for harmony in work is synchronicity. It is the alignment of our spontaneous work with the demand in the environment. The Greek philosopher Aristotle said, "Where your talents and the needs of the world cross, there lies your vocation." The choice of vocation is not an easy one in a society in which such a choice is guided by many extraneous considerations such as money, security, and social prestige. Dream jobs that have all of these and yet are fulfilling are difficult to come by. So most of us make compromises, thereby stifling the inner voice that wants fulfillment in something else. But leaders make precisely those choices that are self-consistent and can bring them fulfillment. To begin with, these choices may not receive popular approval, but leaders follow their inner convictions nevertheless and end up being pioneers. Had Isaac Newton listened to his mother's advice about what he should do in life, he would have ended up running the family farm. We would have then not have had Newton, the scientist who revolutionized the way we look at our world.

The third rule of Einstein is, in the middle of difficulty lies opportunity. If we clearly analyze the ingredients of any difficult situation, we come to understand that the real knot of the difficulty lies more in ourselves than in the situation outside. A champion mountaineer will tell you that the greater difficulty lies not in the steep slope that he negotiates but in the fear in his own heart. Someone involved in car racing is worried not so much about a difficult bend as she is about the steadiness of her nerves.

All difficulties call for a greater surge of energy in one's self. They call for greater involvement. Difficulties challenge us to invoke our higher capacities for thought and action. Sometimes, on the face of it, a difficult situation may appear insurmountable. But if we can hold on to ourselves in the middle of difficulties, we emerge triumphant. The well known British dramatist, George Bernard Shaw wrote (*Mrs. Warren's Profession*, 1893): "The people who get on in this world are the people who get up and look for the circumstances they want, and, if they can't find them, make them."

MODERN MISCONCEPTIONS ABOUT WORK

If we were to visualize our world as a limitless field of action, which it indeed is, our work would seem like a narrow, artificial boundary created by us. When you finish a job successfully and exclaim: "I have done a great job today," do you realize that your claim to greatness does not acknowledge many other contributions toward your triumph? Do you acknowledge, for example, the following contributors to your success: the employer who gave you the job, your old college teacher who taught you the skills necessary for it, your mother, who brought you to this earth, your father, who paid your way through school, the compassionate colleague who helped you out in distress, the old farmer in South America who produced the breakfast cereal you ate in the morning, the orange tree in Florida whose fruit nourished you? If you did not acknowledge all of them and many more, perhaps your statement, "I have done a great job," is only partially true.

What we define as our work is, more often than not, merely an idea that has little connection with reality. In the highly specialized workplace of today, our thinking has become more and more object driven. As a result we have begun to snap our contact with our subjective selves—the meaning we derive from our work and the relevance of our work to our universal concerns.

Our work is an expression of a universal field of action. Even the smallest job we do, such as cleaning the garden, invariably alters the face of the earth. Yet we create an artificial definition (i.e., making finite) out of an infinite dimension of our work. From this crisis of vision, arises the following misconceptions about our work:

Misconception 1: Our Work Is Equivalent to Our Qualifications In many of my workshops, participants introduce themselves as: "I am an engineer" or "I am an accountant," or "ear-nose-throat specialist," or some such qualification. To explore the element of truth implicit in the statement, "I am an engineer," one may ask the following: "Am I an engineer, or have I an engineering qualification? Obviously, my identity as a human being in this world and society is much larger than an engineering degree." One of the maladies of a highly specialized society is that our worldview is often shaped and dominated by our skills at work. Sometimes our worldview shrinks so much that we begin to see ourselves as impersonal mechanisms of an economic engine.

Misconception 2: Our Work Is a Nine-to-Five Affair One great illusion that we love to hold on to is that our work lasts merely from nine in the morning to five in the evening, after which we go home. The truth is that our entire existence is nothing but work. The very fact of our being alive is ample testimony that we are at work whether we are breathing in or breathing out, working our muscles or our minds, working for ourselves or in spite of ourselves. Taking into account the amount of work Nature does to keep us going (maintaining our heartbeats, for example) would convince us that our work is not temporal but is existential.

Misconception 3: Our Work Is Product Not a Process Often what we do is perceived, defined, and measured in terms of an external product of our efforts. Yet all significant work is really an intrinsic process of unfoldment of human consciousness. Even the most tangible product of our work is really a process. The men who toiled to invent the first balloon must have marveled at their creation as humanity's final triumph over gravity. If only they had lived to see our most sophisticated rocket, they would have no problems visualizing that the balloon was only a small and visible product in an unending and invisible process of mankind's inner quest for perfection. Neil Armstrong exclaimed on setting foot on the moon (July 20, 1969): "That's one small step for a man, one giant leap for mankind."

So it is with all our work. We become caught in the product or in the "idea" of the product, so much so that the process remains obscure to our limited vision. The glib, oft-heard expression, "mind over matter," exposes the limitation of a vision that sees the conquest of external Nature by the mind as the only worthwhile work in this world.

On the contrary, the classical wisdom of the East enshrined in the Vedantic and Buddhist texts has emphatically stated the need to conquer internal human nature as a precondition for human development. This assumption is based on direct experiencing or "seeing" by the countless sages and seers of antiquity that mind itself is matter and that it is necessary to conquer the mind and its frailties. Edmund Hillary, the first person to reach the peak of Mount Everest rightly said: "It is not the mountains we conquer, but ourselves."

THE MISSING LINK: SPIRIT IN ACTION

Our industrial civilization has superimposed its own limitations on the cosmic field of action. It has narrowed our views of work to an economically driven, production-focused activity that apparently has no link with the nature and spirit of our being. Any mental or physical activity that is not rooted in the spirit of action alienates workers from their work. Such work, whatever its magnitude, is like a skyscraper without a foundation that is laid low by the first high wind.

Most of our dialogues and discussions around our work surprisingly bypass this spiritual dimension of work and its role in setting right the existential vacuum that afflicts most modern workers. How often have we heard people say: "My work means very little to me. I do not know why I am doing what I am doing." Yet in contemporary managerial parlance, the notion of the spirit has crept in almost unnoticed. We may examine the etymologic roots of the following expressions from the vocabulary of industrial organizations as evidence of what I am trying to convey:

Professional management. The word *profession* is synonymous with the German word *Beruf*, which means religious vocation or calling. It was because of Martin Luther that the German word meaning *profession* took on a spiritual color and passed on from Germany to other Protestant countries. It is only recently that the expression *professional* has lost its spiritual roots and has come to mean work done in return for money.

Charismatic leadership. The *Oxford English Dictionary* defines the word *charisma* as (1) spiritual grace, (2) capacity to inspire devotion and enthusiasm.

Esprit de corps. This expression literally means "the spirit of loyalty and devotion that unites members of a group."

Team spirit. The word *spirit* is so obvious in the expression *team spirit* that we sometimes forget that team building is not only a matter of techniques but also has something to do with our spiritual dimension.

Organizational mission. Organizations on the threshold of the twenty-first century still swear by mission statements. The word *mission* conveys the sense of "guiding light for action." The mission of an organization is nothing but an ideal for channeling the collective spirit of the members of the organization.

The issue of leadership cannot quite ignore the notion of spirit in action. Leaders can act the way they do simply because they are possessed by a spiritual force that makes them believe something inside them is more powerful than their circumstances. Mother Teresa, talking about her life of service, wrote (*Total Surrender*, 1985): "The true interior life makes the active life burn forth and consume everything."

All great leaders nurture their inner spirits in silence and solitude. They are unwavering in their commitment to their chosen ideals. Like Martin Luther King, Jr., they all nourish their dreams. After years of inner preparation, when they emerge on the public arena of life, their indomitable spirits carry them forward. All their actions bear the unmistakable imprints of their spirits. The spirit that we are talking about here is not an abstract phenomenon. It is the power of the integral Self. When leaders become totally integrated with their deepest urges in body, mind, and soul, their spirits are like a coherent beam of laser light—intense and irresistible. They move masses on the wings of this spirit. This is the secret of their charisma.

WORKSHIP: WORK AS WORSHIP

To convey the spiritual essence of an action, the ancient psychologists of India often used a word that does not have a literal translation in English. The word they used was *karmayoga*. This compound word loosely means "work that is linked with the transcendental spirit." My futile search for an equivalent expression in English has prompted me to coin a new word, *workship*. Workship literally means "work as worship." More explicitly, the phrase signifies that when work is done in the spirit of worship, the quality of work undergoes a metamorphosis. As a result, even ordinary work is transformed from a mere chore to an extraordinary reality.

Let us illustrate this with the following example.

Three school teachers who teach history in different schools are asked the same question: What is your present job? The first one replies, "Oh! I don't do very much, I just teach history to school kids." The second person thinks a little more deeply and says, "I am in the business of education." The third person, in response to the same question looks straight into the eyes of the questioner, and in an inspired voice says, "I am shaping the destiny of the nation—I teach young minds how they can make history."

All three teachers are dealing with the same reality—teaching history to school kids. Yet the spirit in which they approach their work transforms the mundane reality of their job.

It is this transformational power of the spirit of our work that leads us to the expression *workship*. The English word *worship* literally means "reverence and respect paid to God." The object of our reverence and respect is not an object at all but is really the ultimate spiritual expression of the highest, the mightiest, and the biggest entity in our conception. Similarly, the objective of our work grows bigger and bigger as we lend our spirit to it. We begin to treat our work with greater reverence and respect until a point is reached when our work becomes an expression of our pure spirit. There is something of the divine perfection in this kind of work. It is then that our work becomes workship. The mystic poet of Persia, Jelaluddin Rumi, expressed the experience of workship in brilliant poetry:

I feel like the ground astonished
at what the sky's spirit has brought to it. What I know
is growing inside me. Rain makes
every molecule pregnant with a mystery.

My definition of *workship* is that it is the performance of action for the unfoldment of the spirit of our being toward greater perfection and higher states of consciousness. This state of perfection is not outside ourselves but is an implicit state of our being. Thus, *workship* implies the following:

1. Workers are fundamentally spiritual beings involved in a human experience; they are not human resources looking for spiritual experience. There is an autonomous, Self-existent spiritual dimension of the human constitution. Our body-mind-

senses framework is only a partial manifestation of the spiritual wholeness that Vedantic psychology describes as the state of *poornatwa*. This state of being can be described as the pure consciousness that is the very ground of our existence. *Poornatwa* is a heightened awareness of our own reality.

2. The ultimate goal of all work is to unfold the essentially spiritual dimension of a human being. Thus the value of work is understood in terms of human development and not merely material output. Max DePree, the retired chief executive officer of Herman Miller, the well known office furniture company, rightly says that the measure of individuals—and so of corporations—is the extent to which we struggle to complete ourselves. Our value, then, can be described as the energy we devote to living up to our potential.

3. The spirit of leaders' actions springs from the nature of their being and its inner foundation in their consciousness. Sri Aurobindo (1977) one of the world's greatest spiritual leaders, explained this process of spiritualization of action in inspiring words: "Change your being, be reborn into the spirit and by that new birth proceed with the action to which the spirit within has appointed you."

4. In *workship* the focus of the leader's action changes from *becoming*, which is a function of external recognition, to *being*, which is a function of consciousness.

LEADERSHIP WORK:
AN ADVENTURE OF CONSCIOUSNESS

Laurence G. Boldt in his book *How to Find the Work You Love* (1993) quotes the ancient Indian sage Rishi Patanjali's thoughts on the creative potential of human consciousness. Patanjali composed the *Yogasutra*, the first scientific documentation of the principle of Yoga. Patanjali described the power of a consciousness that transcends the barriers of thoughts. This is indeed the power behind a leader's unflagging energy and the secret of his work-life:

When you are inspired by some great purpose, some extraordinary project, all your thoughts break their bounds: Your mind transcends limitations, your consciousness expands in every direction, and you find yourself in a new, great and wonderful world. Dormant forces, faculties and talents become alive, and you discover yourself to be a greater person by far that you dreamed yourself to be.

. . . LAURENCE G. BOLDT,
How to Find the Work You Love, 1993

The essence of leadership work is the transformation in the consciousness of the leader that gives her a new standpoint for action. As described by Patanjali, it is a liberating process that gives the leader a taste of *mukti* (freedom) and *ananda* (joy), which, as the Upanishads tell us, are the highest goals of all work. Mundane work becomes workship when action is linked to a transcendental consciousness.

The adventure of consciousness in workship is nothing but a progressive expansion and unfoldment of the self toward all-encompassing, transcendental Self. When we stop thinking primarily about our limited selves and our own conveniences, we undergo a truly heroic transformation of consciousness. The Upanishads explore this transformational journey in terms of four stages of development of self to Self. These four stages of self-development do not happen in mutually exclusive compartments but overlap in a continuum that forms the mosaic of human consciousness.

The first stage of the self, according to the Upanishads is the *annamaya kosha*, or the physical self made of food. From the standpoint of work, the physical self concerns itself with basic physical needs, such as hunger and shelter. This provides an obvious rationale for work for most human beings.

The second stage is that of the vital self. The Upanishads call it the *pranamaya kosha*. A worker at this level of consciousness desires to bring about an extension of the field of physical activity by means of group affiliation and a sense of belongingness to a larger identity, such as a family or an organization. The vital consciousness, as Sri Aurobindo points out, in his monumental work, *The Life Divine*, as follows (Sobel and Prem, 1991):

> . . . is not satisfied with the physical and objective only, but seeks too a subjective, an imaginative, a purely emotive satisfaction and pleasure. If there was not this factor, the physical mind of man left to itself would live like the animal, accepting his first actual life and its limit as his whole possibility, moving in material Nature's established order and asking for nothing beyond it.

The third stage of human consciousness is *manamaya kosha*, or the mental self. This self concerns itself with intellectual and aesthetically satisfying activity, such as highly skilled work or artistic pursuits. The mental self is our thinking and understanding. It is an intermediary stage in human evolution, a half-light thrown from the Infinite. The mental life is ethical, idealistic, and constantly in pursuit of perfection in work.

The last stage of the self as described by the Upanishads is the *vigyanamaya kosha*, which is the sheath of intelligence. This self encompasses the psychic and spiritual domain of human consciousness. Established in this self, leaders perceive their work as boundaryless activity. The work is not for the sake of the leader but for the world at large. The Sanskrit expression for this kind of work is *lokasamgraha*, selfless work for the welfare of all. Leaders now begin to comprehend the unbounded field of action in which their work is but an expression of infinite intelligence. They see themselves not in isolation to that cosmic intelligence but as an integral part of it. From the vantage point of this self leaders begin to transcend the narrow confines of individualistic concerns to the broader concerns of all humanity.

In the last stage of its journey toward higher consciousness, the self of the leader begins to glimpse the Self. The newly awakened consciousness liberates leaders from their limited notion of themselves as physical-vital-mental frames and transports them to the realm of freedom and joy.

While performing on the field of infinite intelligence, the leader realizes, as the mystic does, that:

He is both the play and the player.

THE FOURFOLD PATHS OF WORKSHIP

There are fourfold paths to leadership work—four road maps as it were, all of which take the leader toward *workship*. All these are inner paths leading to the same destination which is the Self. A samurai once met a sage and asked him about the ways of hell and heaven. The sage looked at him and said sternly, "What! an ordinary soldier like you, how will you ever understand what is heaven or hell!" Immediately, the samurai drew out his sword and was about to kill the sage. Unruffled, the sage looked at the samurai and quietly said: "That Sir, is the gateway to hell." Ashamed of his own action, the samurai bowed before the sage. This time, the sage said: "And this Sir, is the way to heaven."

Discipline Discipline is the first path of workship. In the context of modern organizations, discipline has become synonymous with rules and legalities and manual procedures. We have in most organizations a large paraphernalia of control systems, such as confidential reports and performance appraisal reports, which presumably serve as checks and balances for maintaining disciplined output by employees. At their best, however, these procedures are rules of propriety. At their worst they are ineffective, outward strivings that push under the carpet the crucial issue of loss of faith in self-control. It is almost like recruiting more policemen and hoping that the character of the citizens will improve.

The classical spiritual response to the problem of lack of discipline has been to treat not the symptom but the root of the disease itself—the unruly mind that is the ultimate source of all undisciplined action. Vedantic wisdom uses the Sanskrit word *chittasuddhi* to express the aspect of "purity of perception" as the foundation of all disciplines. *Chittasuddhi* encompasses a wide range of physical and mental purification processes that include right thought, right speech, and right action. The principle behind *chittasuddhi* is beautifully conveyed in the following lines from William Shakespeare:

> This above all: to thine own self be true,
> And it must follow, as the night the day,
> Thou canst not then be false to any man.
> . . . *Hamlet*, Act I, scene iii

To improve the quality in our work-life, it is necessary to probe deep into the original sin—loss of virtue and integrity of the inner Self. The true sense of the word *virtue* is, as the *Oxford English Dictionary* defines it, "the ability to produce a definite result." Therefore *virtue* is synonymous with *effectiveness*, as in the expression, "Do you have faith in the virtue of these herbs to cure diseases?" In the context of the Self, virtue is that discipline that leads to Self-effectiveness.

Shintoism emphasizes *makoto*, literally "roundedness," which connotes inner harmony. Taoist sages seek identification with the great pattern of Nature, the *Tao* and thereby gain *Te*, which means *virtue* or *power*. In Taoism, a few cryptic lines adequately describe the modern organizational syndrome of external discipline:

> When virtue is lost, only then does the doctrine of humanity
> arise. When humanity is lost, only then does the doctrine of right-
> eousness arise. When righteousness is lost, only then arise the
> rules of propriety. Now propriety is a superficial expression of
> loyalty and faithlessness, and the beginning of disorder.
> . . . *Tao Te Ching*

Righteousness Righteousness is the next path toward effective action. Ordinarily, righteousness means ethically right action. Righteous action however is not merely superficial morality. In its true sense, righteous action means acting according to the law of one's being, which the *Bhagavad Gita* describes as *swadharma*. Righteous action also implies that the means used for the performance of action are as important as achieving the end results. Thus doing the right thing assumes as much importance as doing the thing right. In workship an action has no value in itself, it takes its value from the force it represents. All action has a certain purpose behind it. Leadership action is a statement of leadership purpose. In the words of Swami Vivekananda: "Work is inevitable, it must be so. But we must work for the right purpose."

The Sanskrit word *swadharma*, which means the *dharma* of the self, broadly defines the purpose of one's life. For example, it is the *dharma* of the apple tree to produce apples. To expect an apple tree to produce mangoes would be contrary to its *swadharma*. There are several interpretations of the word *dharma*, all of which may help us to clarify what righteousness is all about. One meaning of *dharma* is intrinsic nature of all animate or inanimate matter that obeys Nature's laws. Yet another meaning of *dharma* is "religion." *Dharma* also means "right conduct." The classical Indian advice "act according to your *dharma*" conveys the multiplicity of meanings of righteous action. The *Brihadaranyaka Upanishad* describes the connecting link between action and *swadharma* in memorable poetry:

> You are what your deepest nature is.
> As your nature, so is your will.
> As your will is, so is your deed.
> As your deed is, so is your destiny.
> . . . *Brihadaranyaka Upanishad*

Sacrifice Sacrifice is the third dimension of leadership work. This is a word that has acquired a negative connotation in everyday usage. The sacrifice that we are talking about in the context of leadership work does not diminish the self but extends the boundary of the self by giving up the lower for the cause of the higher. The *Bhagavad Gita* talks about the psychological sacrifice in terms of self-control and self-discipline that leads to higher Self-possession and Self-knowledge. Thus a leader who sacrifices small pleasures on the way and drives to work on time everyday acquires the virtue of punctuality, which benefits not only himself but also his organization.

All great religions of the world have conceived work as sacrifice. The Gospel of John reads: "Truly, truly, I say to you, unless a grain of wheat falls into the earth and dies, it remains alone; but if it dies it bears much fruit."

In the sense in which the Bible uses it, sacrifice is a search for the sacred and subtle dimension of life. The grain of wheat sacrifices only its present form to the soil and in turn gets back from the soil a longer lease on life by becoming a part of the larger crop cycle. Leaders similarly sacrifice material forms of life only to attain to something larger than life.

The concept of sacrifice has entered the textbook of all religions through Nature's manuscript, in which we see the enactment of work as sacrifice as a ceaseless law of existence. The biologic food chain is Nature's sacrifice of itself for evolution of higher forms life. So it is with human nature and human life— our work today is a sacrifice for the survival and sustenance of our posterity. I once saw the following words inscribed on the tomb of an Indian soldier who sacrificed his life for his country: *I give up my today for your better tomorrow.*

The Holy Qur'an (108:1-2) relates sacrifice to abundance, which connotes a larger-than-life quest of workship: "Lo! we have given you abundance; so pray to your Lord, and sacrifice."

In the context of leadership, the link between sacrifice and abundance is not abstract but is as real as it can be. A leader who voluntarily takes over the responsibility of a subordinate who is physically unwell or emotionally down on a particular day does indeed sacrifice her precious time and energy. But in real terms what she gains is character and credibility among her followers. Character and credibility do not diminish in time like material resources. They obey the law of abundance by growing in time and spreading in space. The many small sacrifices of the leader snowball into a subtle power—the power of a purposive life. A life of purpose grapples with a higher law of Nature—a law that transcends the life of a single human being and embraces humanity at large. In the words of Will Durant (Boldt, 1993):

> To have a great purpose to work for, a purpose larger than our-selves, is one of the secrets of making life significant, for then the meaning and worth of the individual overflow his personal bor-ders and survive his death.

Transcendence Transcendence is the final step in workship. This is a state of realization in action. What do leaders realize in the middle of action? They cannot realize that which does not exist in reality. What leaders can and do realize is a higher order of reality of their own Selves. This reality infuses the smallest of a leader's actions with grandeur and beauty. "You must watch my life," Gandhi said, "how I live, eat, sit, talk, behave in general. The sum total of all those in me is my religion." Transcendence in the context of leadership does not mean transcendence of action; it simply means the transcendence of self to Self while in action. Star performers experience the ecstasy of transcendence whether they are making music or building an organization.

It is through work as worship that individual conscious-ness transcends its own limitations and attains a higher plane of reference, which is another name for God. The state of transcen-dence is a realization of the creative principle of Nature that works in a quiet, unobtrusive way through our veins, through our heartbeats, through the perfectly synchronized movement of the planets. Charles Lindbergh wrote the following:

> Our restricted senses blind us to the atom's magnitude. Who can look at a stone and comprehend its spinning planetary systems? An iron needle aligns itself with the poles a hemisphere away. In man's present stage, he can neither see the tempo of the atoms nor feel the pulse of epochs, but his understanding can be enhanced through merging imagination with scientific knowledge.
> ... CHARLES A. LINDBERGH, *Autobiography of Values*, 1978

Leaders can comprehend the emergence of great principles in apparently small things. They see larger processes behind small events. All these because they have experienced transcendence in their own lives. They have seen life as a uniting principle beyond the dualities of pleasure and pain, success and failure, the worker and the work. A quiet, still wisdom dawns on these leaders as they realize that they are instruments of a larger purpose of life. The *Bhagavad Gita* describes this state of transcendence as *nirdwanda stithaprajna*, a state of equilibrium of consciousness beyond the stress and dualities of work-life. In Shintoism, the *Oracle of Sumiyoshi* describes the transcendental state of a leader in these beautiful lines:

> I have no corporeal existence
> But universal benevolence is my divine body
> I have no physical power
> But uprightness is my strength
> I have no religious clairvoyance beyond
> What is bestowed by wisdom
> I have no power of miracle other than
> The attainment of quiet happiness
> I have no tact except
> The exercise of gentleness.

IS WORKSHIP WORKABLE?

Workship not only is a philosophical construct but also is based on the experiential learning and the collective wisdom of many men and women of the world. Gandhi and Mother Teresa are not quirks of history. They represent a glorious continuum of human beings who have time and again proved to us the efficacy of workship as an alternative to the need- and greed-based contemporary models of work.

As a country, Japan has demonstrated a national model of workship. Much of modern scholarship tends to explain the Japanese economic miracle in terms of stereotypes such as pan-nationalism, work-culture, *kaizen*, and total quality management. Contemporary historians and sociologists, however, are coming out with increasing evidence of a spiritual basis of the Japanese economic resurgence. Ronald Robertson wrote:

I suggest that there are two relatively unique features of Japanese religion which have a great bearing upon these puzzles and which, at the same time, make it necessary to speak of Japanese religion as being a cohesive, relatively autonomous whole in spite of its superficial heterogeneity. I refer first, to the particular nature of Japanese *syncretism* and second to the resilience of what I call the *infrastructural significance of religion itself*. I also invoke the significance of pollution/purification rituals throughout Japan's history, rituals which are central to the native Shinto tradition.

. . . RONALD ROBERTSON,
Globalization: Social Theory and Global Culture, 1992

Another Western analyst named Wolferen (1989) argued that the ideology of "Japaneseness" consists in the overall religious attributes of the Japanese system and that religion in Japan is closely interwoven with the enigma of Japanese power. Thus it does seem that the superstructure of Japanese work-life is being gradually linked with Japan's spiritual and religious-cultural infrastructure.

In the global context we find that a consumption-based model of work has posed a threat to the viability of our ecologic system. The blueprint of this impending disaster lies in the ecology of our egocentric minds. The natural resources of the world are fast being depleted and humanity is poised against Nature, which to them is but a "resource" to be exploited.

We must realize that Nature is not an unthinking resource but is an intelligent response system that has its subtle linkage with human destiny. The alienation of human beings from Nature today is only a consequence of their alienation from their own existential identities. To be truly human is to be related through work to this vast and varied richness of Nature's playground. The ancient Indian expression *vasudhaivya kutumbakkam* crystallizes the wisdom of a civilization that looked on the whole world as one community. Workship attempts this linkage between human beings and their cosmic identities, which have been ruptured largely in the course of three centuries of industrialization. This model of work has great significance for sustainable world development.

Workship also is a radical shift in paradigm from the Greek concept of work as *ponos* (pain) or "labor" to one of striving toward *ananda* (joy) and *mukti* (freedom). This shift in consciousness lifts the anchors of work from a mundane, meaningless routine and gives it an exalted status. Leaders have a debt to their destinies to unfold that dimension of their human potential that makes work a liberating experience.

Workship, as stated earlier, is a leader's adventure of consciousness. Like all adventures, the path leading to its destination is beset with surprises at every turn—pleasures and pitfalls, failures and successes, which make all journeys memorable. All adventure have their uniqueness, just as all human beings are unique although they have a common ancestry and a common destiny in birth and death. Yet imagine a leader's surprise when he discovers, after years of traveling that his destination was never apart from him but always was a part of his very being, resting deep within himself, only waiting to be arrived at by means of the magic wings of awareness.

TOWARD EFFORTLESS EFFORT

One of the enigmas of leadership work is the effortlessness with which leaders perform tasks with which ordinary mortals struggle. The countless inventions of Edison, the comic genius of Charlie Chaplain, the magic of Michael Jordan on the basketball court, the boundless compassion of Mother Teresa, the charisma of Mahatma Gandhi—all these seem awe-inspiring to us. Yet to the leaders themselves their action is spontaneous and a natural expression of their talents. As Leonardo Da Vinci, the multifaceted creative genius wrote, "I am never weary of being useful. . . . No labor is sufficient to tire me." Zen Buddhism has a cryptic expression, "effortless effort" to describe this kind of work. *Tao Te Ching*, China's most well-known book of wisdom, advises us:

> Act without doing;
> work without effort.
> . . . *Tao Te Ching*

If we carefully read Nature's manuscript, we can find the secret of effortless effort. I have often watched with a sense of wonder how a flock of birds sweep across the sky like aircraft flying in battle formation. They negotiate windy pathways, swerve in sharp angles, and traverse long distances in the wink of an eye. At the head of the flock is one bird who makes no special effort to lead. It yields place to one of its co-travelers, apparently without any succession trauma. There is a spontaneous sharing of vital energy as the flock moves as a team. The impulse of this energy is shared by each member of the team. The alchemy of collaboration is at work. The formation of the group remains cohesive without any plans. The goal is reached without any roadmap. The leader leads without any fanfare. The birds accomplish their journey effortlessly, leaving no trace on the sky.

If we carefully analyze what is going on in the world of Nature we will realize that effortless effort is possible for the bird and animal and the plant because all of them remain true their intrinsic identities or *swadharma* that we have discussed earlier. The tree does not labor to produce a fruit, the fruit just grows. The bird does not struggle to sing a song, the song just flows from it. What applies to the rest of Nature also applies to human nature. We have certain intrinsic qualities that form part of our physical, mental, and spiritual constitution. These qualities emerge from us with effortless ease. If you ask a man how come he became so tall or a woman how she loves her child so much, they would be baffled by your question. They would recall nothing that they specially did to be tall or loving—they were expressions of their innate nature.

Effortless effort is a function of an integral being. In Chapter 1 I talked about an integral person as someone whose body, mind, and senses orchestrate themselves to the effortless rhythms of the universe. I also said that an integral person begins to experience a spiritual affinity with the natural order of the universe and that his inner Nature becomes one with his outer nature. When such an integral person acts, he does so from the ground of his very being and very existence. His effort is the outcome of the undivided energy of his Self that he is capable of pressing into service.

Gandhi was known to be able to sustain a high level of energy for long periods of time. Most leaders, in fact, seem to possess an inexhaustible storehouse of energy and great capacity for action. This is possible as a great leader is able to focus his entire energy to the process of action without losing sight of the goal at the same time. Ordinary people waste a lot of energy in focusing on the goal by imagining all kinds of possible outcomes. This energy can be transferred to the task at hand that will bring the goal nearer to us. What one is trying to convey here is that while our intention is on the goal, the energy of our attention should be on the process. Swami Vivekananda once said, "Pay attention to the means of work. The end will take care of itself."

Effortless effort is nothing but the science and art of energy conservation. I shall explain this with an example from the corporate world. Two Managers X and Y are competing for a particular leadership position in a corporation. X is very goal-oriented. He is highly imaginative and dreams of his impending success. He is obsessed with the prospects of his promotion and is very anxious to know whether he would get it at the end of the year. On the other hand Y is introspective and concentrates more on her work rather than on its possible outcome. She is not as power-driven as X but is intensely focused on her work. She would also like to assume the position that X is aspiring for but she does not fantasize about it. Now, let us explore the possible psychological states of X and Y under the following circumstances:

Circumstance # 1. *X is promoted instead of Y* : In this circumstance X will be ecstatic as his dream has come true. He is very likely to beat his chest and raise his arms like a football star and say, "See, I did it!" Y would be disappointed, of course. But since she did not invest too much psychological energy on the goal, she will be sad for a while and resume her work, saying "I must work harder and find out where my deficiencies are."

Circumstance # 2. *Y is promoted instead of X* : In this case, X's world is likely to come crashing down. He had pinned so much hope on this promotion, invested so much psychological energy in it (in fantasizing how happy his wife would be; how he will spend the raise in salary in buying a new car and so on). He is furious with his boss for not promoting him and remains sullen and angry with his colleagues for days together. On the other hand Y is obviously happy with her promotion. But since her focus has been more on her work, she tells herself, "I must have done my job well. However, I must do still better in the future."

Circumstance # 3. *Neither X nor Y are promoted.* We have already discussed the impact of failures on X and Y. It will be clear to us that since Y is more focused on the process rather than on the outcome, she is more likely to handle failures better and be better equipped to face further challenges than X.

Now, we know that in a competitive society, we are engaged in many competing situations in many fields of endeavor. If X and Y both find themselves in many such "races of life" where failures and successes come to both, we will see that X is likely to emerge a chronic complainer at every instance of failure. He will also be disproportionately delighted at his successes. Y will emerge as a more balanced person, learning from successes and failures and transcending both towards greater and greater perfection. It is very likely that Y will be a true leader in her field of action.

Commenting on the quality of our modern work-life where competition often leads to the process of de-humanization of people, a frustrated executive once said, "The trouble with the rat race is that even if you win you are still a rat." It is a well established fact that competition among products or services of similar nature improves the quality of the product and the efficiency of service. But, what is true of a product or service may not be true in the case of human development.

Some of the ills of competitive rivalry are crudely manifest in organizations of today in the form of excessive stress, jealousy, back-biting, burnout syndrome, and a whole host of allied problems. The only antidote to these diseases is to be able to offset the imbalance that excessive competition produces in our psychological constitution by nurturing our spirit of cooperation.

The competitive instinct manifests itself when we look at our work from the standpoint of our ego. The cooperative instinct is an outcome of our empathy with "the other." Talking about competition in contemporary American society, Martin Luther King, Jr. said that as a society we are prone to judge our successes by the index of our salaries or the size of our automobiles rather than by the quality of our service and relationship to one another.

If we could measure the amount of energy that we waste in upholding our own self-image in the eyes of society, we would readily come to the conclusion that after a certain point in time, the competitive self becomes an inefficient self. The sense of anxiety that we carry with us in maintaining the illusion of our success and affluence is indeed energy-dissipating. The same energy that we waste in maintaining our separateness in a competitive setup can bring great joy in a cooperative framework. Mahatma Gandhi told us the secret of cultivating the constructive energy of cooperation by nurturing the spirit of service, as follows:

> Consciously or unconsciously, every one of us does render some service or other. If we cultivate the habit of doing this service deliberately, our desire for service will steadily grow stronger, and will make, not only for our own happiness, but for the world at large.

The *Bhagavad Gita* describes effortless effort as *nishkam karma*. Work that is freed from the bondage of our egocentric self is *nishkam karma*. Work that does not encounter the defenses of our desire has the power of an arrow that is unleashed from the confines of the bow. Work that becomes workship operates on the principle of least resistance and therefore is of greater efficiency. Buddha's description of effortless effort is simple, as follows:

> Sit
> Rest
> Work.
> Alone with yourself,
> Never weary.
> On the edge of the forest
> Live joyfully,
> Without desire.

The Bible urges us to follow the economy of effort in Nature's work: "Consider the lilies of the field, how they grow; they toil not, neither do they spin. And yet I say unto you, That even Solomon in all his glory was not arrayed like one of these" (Matthew 6:28–29).

Leaders are the ones who bring a surge of energy and a sense of rhythm into the arena of action. The execution of their work has the flawlessness of a Nature' masterpiece. Leaders excel because of the quality of their service. The only ones among us who will be truly fulfilled in our work are those who have sought and found how to serve. The search for a true vocation is to learn how we can best serve the world. Leadership is a natural outcome of this search.

4

Leadership and Organization

ORGANIZATION: THE ALCHEMY OF COLLABORATION

Organizations are not human inventions. They are neither the outcome of hummankind's crafty thinking nor quite the marvels of our industrial, technological civilization, as we often tend to believe. The story of organizations is to be found in Nature's manuscript—the unwritten book of nature that scripts in vivid details the fundamental quest of all life forms to manifest their fullest potential for collective action.

A honeycomb is a realization of the organizational instinct inherent in bees. The basic design of the honeycomb is an intricate hexagonal structure that slopes at a precise angle of thirteen degrees to the horizontal. It is an act of sophisticated civil engineering that prevents honey from running out. Bees also demonstrate the air-conditioning mechanism implicit in natural intelligence by crowding themselves into a dense mass when the honeycomb is made. The temperature of this mass is held constant between thirty-four and thirty-five degrees Celsius, which is necessary for secretion of wax. All these happen as the unerring instinct of the bee begins to orchestrate itself with the laws of Nature. The honeycomb is not a building that is laboriously constructed brick by brick. It is an outcome of spontaneous creation, a piece of brilliant architecture that emerges from the blueprint of conscious nature.

When we analyze the anatomy of one individual bee, we see that there is nothing sophisticated in its cellular structure—at least not the kind of sophistication that is required to invent and design a structure as complex as a honeycomb. When these ordinary bees get together, however, there is a unique alchemy of collaboration. The secret of this alchemy lies in an undefinable energy that possesses the bees when they come together. In human organizations, this undefinable element is often referred to as *synergy.*

The functioning of the human body is another example of this kind of alchemy at work. The body has many different functional components, such as the nervous system, the respiratory system, the circulatory system, and the digestive system. The functional complexity of each of these systems is much greater than any high-tech unit of industrial organization. The various organs of the body, such as the heart, liver, and kidneys, serve as the hub of activity within a particular system. In short, everything that constitutes the organization of the body is geared toward one organizational goal—to maintain the body in a state of health. The body achieves this goal through a unique process known as *homeostasis.*

Homeostasis refers to the extraordinary chemical and physiologic equilibrium that the body maintains to preserve the conditions of life. In one of his essays on the theme of *homeostasis,* Dr. Walter Cannon wrote the following:

> When we consider the extreme instability of our bodily structure, its readiness for disturbance by the slightest application of external forces and the rapid onset of its decomposition as soon as favoring circumstances are withdrawn, its persistence through

many decades seems almost miraculous. The wonder increases when we realize that the system is open, engaging in free exchange with the outer world.

> . . . WALTER CANNON, *Wisdom of the Body*, 1963

Even a minuscule increase in the sugar or salt level or even the temperature in the body is capable of upsetting its health. Yet the human organism maintains its resilience against all odds through the principle of *homeostasis*. One of the unsolved enigmas of medical science is the invisible source of intelligence that maintains the vitality and balance of the body under adverse circumstances. The sixteenth-century physician Paracelsus defined as follows the role of the physician in terms of making sense of this invisible dimension of the human body:

> The physician should speak of that which is invisible. What is visible should belong to his knowledge, and he should recognize the illness, just as everybody else, who is not a physician, can recognize them by their symptoms. But this is far from making him a physician; he becomes a physician only when he knows that which is unnamed, invisible and immaterial, yet efficacious.

The physicians of ancient India described this invisible element that brought about the alchemy of collaboration within the human body as *prana*. In the general sense of the word, *prana* refers to the life principle. It also denotes energy, vital breath, power, or the animating force of the cosmos. The body is looked on by these physicians as a microcosmic expression of cosmic vitality. *Prana* is the essence of the synergy of the body; it is the conscious intelligence that informs every cell of the body that it is part of a larger whole. This intercellular intelligence is what acts as a glue to the organization of the human body.

In many ways, organizations resemble the working of a human body. The theory of organization as an organism is not a new one. But most of the sociological studies in this respect have ignored the invisible element of conscious intelligence that pervades any organization or organism. The synergy among members of a particular organization is not merely a physical stringing together of people like beads in a necklace. There is a spiritual affinity (as in team spirit) that connects one member of a team or an organization with another.

Each member of an organization possesses the capacity for synergy, just as each cell of the human body possesses the intelligence of the entire body. In other words, we may say that each member of the organization has the emergent intelligence that brings the organization into being. I am using the word *emergent* in the sense that the ability to organize does not emerge in a member until he or she finds himself or herself in a group. Synergy in human organizations is an outcome of group dynamics in much the same way that the dynamic interaction of a group of bees brings about the energy and intelligence required to create a beehive.

ORGANIZATION AS A COMMUNITY

Before industrial organizations came into being in the last couple of centuries, the most powerful forms of organizations were communities—religious, social, and cultural groups that shared common interests and were alike in some way or another. Unlike modern organizations, however, communities were driven not by bottom lines and profits but by a common purpose. The relation between members of a community were of two kinds: horizontal and vertical. The horizontal relationship was based on tasks that the community members performed together. The vertical relationship was in the community members' commitment to a common cause, which was either serving God or serving the community spirit or some such supramundane entity.

In corporations of today, horizontal relationships are fairly well-defined and nurtured by devices such as quality circles and team-building exercises. However, the vertical relationship that consists in searching for a common spirit or purpose has almost disappeared from the agenda of modern organizations. The result has been reduction of work to an economic goal and growing disenchantment of people with what they do in their factories and offices.

Corporations and communities may exist for different purposes, but the common ground between them is that they are made up of human beings; they are run by human beings and are meant to serve human needs and aspirations. Human beings do not live only on lateral relationships with peers and superiors at work. They search for the vertical purpose of their existence in this grand cosmic scheme of which they are integral parts. The efficiency of the modern corporation and the efficacy of traditional communities must come together if organizations of today are to have any chance at survival. A community without the drive and discipline of a modern corporation becomes an ineffective coalition of fun lovers. A corporation without the liberating spirit of the community becomes a vicious circle of cold-hearted fortune seekers.

Yet another dimension that binds a community and a corporation together is good leadership. The issue of leadership was as much a concern in traditional communities as it is in present-day corporations. The traditional Buddhist communities have the following common prayer:

Buddham sharanam gacchami
Dharmam sharanam gacchami
Sangham sharanam gacchami

The first line translates as "I remember the Buddha and affirm my allegiance to Him." The second line means, "I remember and affirm my allegiance to the principle of *dharma*, of which the Buddha is the upholder." The third line says, "I affirm my allegiance to the organization, or *sangha*, which is the embodiment of the Buddha." Thus we see a clear prioritization of commitments of the members of the Buddhist communities.

The first of these commitments is to the leader, the Buddha who is the embodiment of the principle of the organization (*dharma*) as well as the organizational structure (*sangha*). In the leader, the traditional communities saw the manifestation of the highest purpose of their lives. The Buddha, for them, was not so much a physical person as He was an embodiment of truth, love, and compassion. The Buddha is for the Buddhists the ultimate human destiny—the very purpose of the organization to which they dedicate themselves.

We can clearly see that in a community the lateral relationship between the members has no value in itself. This relationship derives its value from a vertical relationship with the leader. The leader is therefore vested with the responsibility of not only heading the institution but also of being a person who is committed to the principles on which the organization is built. The relationship between the leader and the organization is not contractual but is integral. In the context of communities, leaders cannot lead until they have total integrity to the cause of the organization.

In modern corporations, leaders are seen primarily as strategists whose sole aim seems to be to outwit rival companies to stay in business. Policies and not principles seem to be the guiding light for this kind of leadership. Policies are merely pronouncements and documents that are not integrated with life. Thus leaders who are merely corporate strategists abandon their policies as soon as circumstances change. In today's corporations, we see many examples of leaders who abandon their policies. Their commitment of employment ends up in ruthless retrenchment when profits dip. Equality of employment opportunity is violated with creation of invisible glass ceilings for minority and women employees. Chief executive officers continue to take astronomical salaries even when they downsize employees for austerity measures. Gandhi, who himself led with principles, once said that leading with policies is not an authentic test of leadership because if a leader says that "honesty is the best policy," he implies that if it were not the best policy under certain circumstances, he would abandon honesty.

While leading the Indian community of several million toward independence, Gandhi based his leadership principle on the notion of *trusteeship*. This principle was an outcome of his understanding of the leadership role as one of a trustee responsible for keeping in trust the power given by followers. Trusteeship acknowledges the fact that the power, position, and influence of leaders come to them because of the trust that followers have in their leaders. Therefore, leaders are responsible for using their positions, not for personal interest but in the interest of the larger communities that has made them the leaders.

Leaders in today's industrial organizations have to understand the deep implications of trusteeship as a principle of effective leadership. Trusteeship upholds the value of relationship in leadership work. Leadership is not a position or a rank; it is primarily and fundamentally a relationship of trust between leader and follower. The more leaders honor this trust, the greater will be their credibility with their followers and the more effective their leadership will be.

If modern corporations acknowledge the fact that they are like traditional communities in more ways than one, then we will begin to see a new tradition emerging in business. With increasing globalization of businesses we are witnessing a countermovement of localization of business cultures. This is a movement toward recognition of the values of a community. Reuben Mark, former chief executive officer of Colgate Palmolive, talking about this trend in *Fortune* magazine said the following:

> Setting up in new countries is different from how it used to be. Once, you dropped an American off in Venezuela or Thailand with a boatload of toothpaste and had him build a business. Now we go into partnership with local business people or the local government. The fundamental difficulty is how to execute a global strategy and still allow those leading the local entity to feel they are controlling their own destiny. We encourage them to be entrepreneurial so they can feel responsible for their results.
>
> . . . REUBEN MARK, *Fortune*, March 26, 1990

The community nature of modern organizations is emerging in business practices such as "think globally, act locally." Business leaders the world over are beginning to understand that leadership in business is built on relationships—not only horizontal relationships of convenience but also vertical relationships of commitment to the community in which the business operates. Leadership in a community comes from the creative explorations of the nature and organization of relations within a community and from honoring these relationships in speech, thought, and action.

ORGANIZATIONS: FROM CONSTRUCTION TO CREATION

In trying to understand the nature of human organizations, one ought to make a distinction between creation and construction. Whereas creation is a living process, construction is a finished or unfinished structure of frozen life. Creation is multidimensional and dynamic; construction is sequential, progressing step by step. A tree growing from a seed is creation; a building rising from its foundation is construction.

In the tree the form emerges from inside out; in the building the form is given shape from outside in. When a small plant emerges from the soil, there is something very magical about it. The tiny twig is already an entire structure of multicellular compartments complete with interconnections of intercellular intelligence and painted a soothing shade of green. During the creation of a plant, the intelligence inherent in the seed performs a multiple and simultaneous range of functions with effortless ease. In construction, parts are added to conform to an idea of the whole. In creation, it is the whole that conceives, manifests itself, and becomes the whole. Creation is the emergence of the whole as the whole.

Any human organization has both a creative aspect and a constructive aspect. Whereas the energy and vision of its members constitute the creative element of an organization, the functional division of the organization into design, manufacturing, and marketing constitutes the constructive element. Creation provides the organization with its core impulse, or the spirit of enterprise. Construction provides the tools and mechanisms for channeling impulse into activity.

Creation and construction have to maintain a fine balance if the organization has to remain healthy. Obsessive focus on construction—structures, systems and procedures—constricts the life-breath of the organization, bureaucratize it, and suffocates it. Whereas the creative energy of an organization is the invisible domain of organizational life, it is nevertheless real. We often confuse invisibility with nonreality and forget to nurture the subtle elements of organized activity such as trust, integrity, and cooperative spirit. When neglected, these invisible aspects become visible as symptoms of organizational disease such as rapid turnover, excessive bureaucratization, and the spawning of a culture of sycophancy.

Managers often find it tempting to tamper too much with the constructive element of organizations. The reason is obvious—it gives greater visibility to their management functions and brings greater rewards. A designer is obsessed with an exotic design that will show the designer as a performer irrespective of the value of the design to the organization. Similarly, a production manager is fixated with production figures without bothering to find out whether it is possible to achieve better quality of the products within given parameters.

Often the process of construction of organizations leads to rigid constructs. These constructs are nothing but ideas or perceptions that result from repeated sense impressions. Take the example of a performance review system introduced in an organization by an external consultant employed by a chief executive officer.

> *The chief executive officer, who had experience in the army, was inclined to change the existing two-page performance review form to a longer one with greater provision for supervision and control. The consultant duly complied with the request and produced a ten-page form that soon replaced the existing one. The initial enthusiasm of the personnel department in introducing the new tool was evident. The personnel staff fed the chief executive officer with exaggerated reports of the effectiveness of the new tool and reinforced the infallibility of her command and control system of management.*
>
> *The accumulation of selective positive feedback about her management style produced a construct, or mind map, that prompted the chief executive officer to disregard such symptoms of organizational disease as increasing employee resentment and absenteeism. As time passed, the chief executive officer discovered that "ordering around" was resulting*

*in anger and hostility among employees and stoppage of information
flow from the junior staff. The chief executive officer began to question
unrealistic assumptions that went into her construct and blocked the
perception of reality.*

Most chief executive officers become acutely aware of the
nonfunctional corpses of their constructs, but very few are wise
enough to enliven their frozen mental maps with the creative
impulse of their consciousness. Instead, most chief executive
officers search for solutions in other constructs, alternative mind
maps, and quick-fix consultants to repair the nonfunctioning
part of the organization or replace it with a new model. This is
an easy way out, because it saves chief executive officers the
pain involved in confronting their deeply ingrained beliefs and
in learning to clear the cobwebs of their own minds. Leadership
divorced from learning reduces a leader to an anachronistic
mechanism who like the proverbial man with a hammer
assumes the whole world is a nail.

LEADERSHIP IN A LEARNING ORGANIZATION

He who would, may reach the utmost height—but he must be
eager to learn.

Learning is as old as civilization itself. When human beings first
learned to use fire, a entirely new vista of possibilities for action
opened to civilization. Food was cooked, metals were forged
into tools, and darkness was dispelled even after sunset. The
one leader who discovered fire pushed the evolutionary urge of
all civilization. As recognized by the first person to set foot on
the moon, that single step was the beginning of a giant stride for
the progress of humankind.

In the context of leadership, learning may be described as
building capacity for action. This capacity for action does not
come merely from knowledge; it comes from learning. We must
differentiate between knowledge and learning. Knowledge is the
process of accumulating information or experience in a given

context. Thus knowledge is an event. Learning, on the other hand, is movement of knowledge beyond an event. Learning is a continuous process. Take the discovery of fire by a certain member of the human species on one particular day. This discovery did not end in an event in which one person acquired the knowledge of how to start a fire. Rather, this event triggered in the consciousness of this one person a process of further discoveries. Knowledge about the event of a fire gives rise to new learning about the multiple capacities of fire to ignite, illuminate, generate power, and destroy.

To take another example of a person who has the experience of riding a bicycle for the first time. The knowledge acquired about the movement of a bicycle is not an event or even a sequence of events. It is a much more subtle process of learning to balance oneself. The event of moving on a bicycle gives the rider an intuitive understanding and a sense of dynamic balance. This sense of balance was already there, the rider discovered it only by relating external knowledge to herself.

Learning is not merely capacity building, it is the capacity building in one's self. Learning is the process of self-knowing. Knowledge of external reality is merely a stimulus. Learning is transformation in the self in response to this stimulus. Learning is not a mechanical picking up of bits and pieces of data from the environment; it is the creative and continuous processing of this information within the self. When knowledge deepens into learning, the self acquires the capacity for creative action.

To draw on the example of learning to ride a bicycle, we can see that this learning is a self-generating process. As we learn the generic skill of balancing ourselves on two wheels, we acquire the capacity of riding not only a bicycle but also a motorcycle or for that matter anything that requires this ability to hold the body in a dynamic balance. Or take the case of learning to write. It is a skill that begins with a basic knowledge of the alphabet. Then we know the relationship of one letter with another in a word. Ultimately, when our knowledge deepens into learning how to write, we realize that our capacity to write is intimately linked to ourselves. Writing then becomes a self-generating capacity to express ourselves in many creative ways—prose or poetry or fiction.

Whereas knowledge is the gathering of information, learning is the development of creative intelligence to transform this information into action. Knowledge deals with the *what* of reality; learning deals with the *how* of it. Knowledge is merely classification of information; learning is the ability to draw the energy out of this information into the arena of action. Leaders integrate the what of knowledge with the how of learning. There is total integration between knowledge and action. Napoleon is reported to have said that the word *impossible* never existed in his dictionary ("You write to me that it's impossible; the word is not French," Letter to General Lemarois, July 9, 1813). Between the comprehensible and the possible, there exists no separation in the mind of the leader. Learning in leadership is the ability to see the possible in the comprehensible, to identify that which is actionable in the realm of knowledge. In short, the leader acquires the discipline necessary for converting knowledge into actionable learning.

It is this discipline of learning that separates the true leader from the rest of us. We all know about the value of nonviolence, but it takes the discipline of Gandhi to convert this value into enduring power. We all know that compassion is a great human quality, yet it takes the commitment of Mother Teresa to translate this quality into real life. We all know how wonderful it would be if we had equality in our society, but it takes the zeal of Martin Luther King, Jr., to make that happen.

Leaders acquire the discipline to operationalize knowledge into learning. Their learning is synonymous with action. When Gandhi was thirty-five years of age and living in South Africa, he came across a book called *Unto This Last* by John Ruskin. Ruskin wrote that the liberation of the individual lay in the liberation of the community. This single book transformed Gandhi's life, and he resolved to convert this knowledge into action. In Gandhi's words, "I arose with the dawn ready to reduce these principles into practice" (Fischer, 1962).

Gandhi's described his lifelong learning in his autobiography, *The Story of My Experiments with Truth* (Fischer, 1962). His immense organization building capacity was founded on this one Truth that he had set out to discover—it was the Truth about his own Self:

> What I want to achieve—what I have been striving and pining to achieve these thirty years—is self-realization, to see God face to face, to attain Moksha [liberation]. I live and move and have my being in pursuit of this goal. All that I do by way of speaking and writing, and all my ventures in the political field are directed to this same end.

The sages of India had understood that the ultimate quest of all learning is Self-learning. They called this process *swadhyay*. Self-learning is a neverending process of discovering the foundation of all knowledge. Just think of it—where is all your knowledge about the world processed? Within the Self. You can say that you know about the existence of the sun only because your eyes can see it. You know the law of gravity because your body can feel it. Is any learning possible except within the context of the Self? If you think deeply about it, you will realize that no knowledge exists beyond the Self.

J. Krishnamurti, the renowned spiritual teacher of our times, wrote about his passion for learning as follows:

> I am learning about myself from moment to moment, and the *myself* is extraordinarily vital. It is living, moving; it has no beginning and no end. When I say, "I know myself," learning has come to an end in accumulated knowledge. Learning is never cumulative; it is a movement of knowing that has no beginning and no end.
>
> . . . J. KRISHNAMURTI, *On Learning and Knowledge*, 1994

A leader acquires a great psychological advantage by being in a constant state of Self-learning. But how is this psychological advantage of the leader translated into competitive advantage for the organization. In other words, how does a leader convert individual learning into organizational learning? Peter Senge, who has pioneered the creation of learning organizations throughout the world, redefines the role of the leader in a learning organization as follows:

> Leaders are designers, teachers and stewards. These roles require new skills: the ability to build shared vision, to bring to the surface and challenge prevailing mental models, and to foster more systemic patterns of thinking. In short, leaders in learning organizations are responsible for building organizations where people are continually expanding their capabilities to shape their future—that is, leaders are responsible for learning.
>
> ... PETER M. SENGE, *The Fifth Discipline: The Art and Practice of Learning Organization*, 1990

ORGANIZATIONAL VALUES AND SELF-LEARNING

In the fast-changing knowledge economies of the twenty-first century, Self-learning will be a core competency and continuous learning the only way to survive global competitiveness. But the crucial question is, how does the leader infuse the spirit of learning in the organization? What are the kinds of commitments required for this purpose? What are the organizational values that make continuous learning within the organization a reality? In the next few pages I discuss humility, faith, and total quality consciousness as the three foundational values of learning.

Humility The first step in learning is humility. It is the ground on which knowledge grows into learning. The word *humility* comes from *humus*, or soil. The ground reality or the soil is a state of pure potentiality. The ground is fertile with the intelligence for activating the seed of knowledge into the living process of learning. By convention humility is understood as a social norm or etiquette. In the real sense, however, it is a state of mind. A person is humble not so much because he or she thinks less of himself or herself but because he or she thinks of himself or herself less.

There is a radical difference between the two ways of looking at humility. In the first instance, when we underplay ourselves because it is a social norm, we are being humble in the conventional and more acceptable sense of the word. In this case, we may put an appearance of humility before others but can still be full of thoughts about ourselves and our own importance. On the other hand, if we are truly humble, we learn to reduce the energy that we invest in thinking about our own accomplishments and in upholding our ego. When we take stock of how much of the organizational energy goes to waste upholding our positions and points of view, we realize that we hardly have any energy left to learn anything new.

It sounds paradoxic but it is true that if we want Self-learning, we have to learn to think less about our little selves and their egocentric knowledge. Self-learning comes from suspension of our existing knowledge, which clutters our perspective of life and prevents fresh learning. In organizations many brilliant ideas are shot down by incompetent bosses who seem to "know" that "this can't be done" or "that is too impractical to be implemented." Nothing acts as a greater block to organizational learning than a know-all mental attitude.

In one of my corporate workshops a young executive once asked me: "I do not know and am not very clear about many things relating to my work. Yet, I pretend to know everything because I feel it is the smart thing to do. How can I get rid of this problem of mine?" My response to his question was: "Please find out a little more about the Self who knows that you do not know so much. Your problem would be automatically solved." To quote what I learned from Mother Teresa:

> Self-knowledge puts us on our knees and it is very necessary. . . .
> If you are humble, nothing will touch you, neither praise nor disgrace, because you know what you are. If you are blamed, you won't be discouraged; if anyone calls you a saint, you won't put yourself on a pedestal.
>
> . . . MOTHER TERESA, *Total Surrender*, 1985

Mother Teresa's words put in a nutshell the essence of learning as a dispassionate pursuit of Self-knowledge that is not contaminated by our self-image. The sages of The Upanishads called this kind of knowledge *atma-vidya*, or knowledge of the true Self. *Atma-vidya* is not knowledge in the sense of accumulation of information. It is a continuous process of clarifying the cobwebs of self-image that cloud our Self-knowing. *Atma-vidya* is the ultimate goal of learning, and humility is the starting point.

In the context of creating a learning organization, a leader has to make sure that individual learning also translates into team learning. The value of humility is an essential ingredient of team learning. In teamwork, every member has to suspend judgment about what others know or are capable of knowing. This suspension of judgment ensures more receptivity to learning and allows greater circulation of energy and information within the team. Charles Williams underlined the importance of humility in the context of team learning as follows: "No mind was so good that it did not need another mind to counter and equal it, and to save it from conceit and blindness and bigotry and folly. Only in such a balance could humility be found" (Williams, 1965).

Faith The second important value on which a learning organization is built is faith or trust. Trust is only a consequence of faith. Organizations such as the Missionaries of Charity, the Salvation Army, and the Ramkrishna Mission are built purely on faith. Truly speaking no organization can survive, let alone learn, without faith. I have often asked these questions of myself: Is there any one thing I learned in my life that did not begin with faith?

How did I learn the alphabet? Because I had faith in my parents, whom I trusted. How did I learn mathematics and geography? I had faith in my teachers. I still learn new things simply because I have faith in my ability to learn.

What is true of individual learning is true of organizational learning. Organizations that have intrinsic faith in their capacity to create their own destiny learn faster than their counterparts. Leadership within the organization is responsible for instilling this self-fulfilling faith among the members of the organization. Sometimes this process is referred to as the *Pygmalion effect* in management. The Pygmalion effect is the direct result of expanding the learning capacity of the organization by removing organizational blocks to learning, such as fear of punishment for making mistakes and extreme centralization of the decision-making process.

Fear of making mistakes can prove costlier to organizations than the mistakes themselves. Leaders who value organizational learning as a leverage point for organization development accommodate even costly mistakes of their employees for the long-term benefit of the organization. I once heard the following wonderful story about an IBM chief executive.

> *An employee of IBM made a very expensive error, which lead to a revenue loss of several million dollars. Shaking with fear at the enormity of his mistake, the employee typed out his resignation letter and brought it to the chief executive officer. The chief executive looked at the letter and shouted back, "What on earth makes you feel we will dismiss you after we have spent so much on your education!"*

How does one define faith in the context of learning? Rabindranath Tagore (1955) wrote: "Faith is the bird that feels the light and sings when the dawn is still dark." Faith is the ability to process one's intuitive intelligence—it is a knack for figuring things out even when there is inadequate data support. The leader who can perceive the emerging patterns of organizational reality much ahead of his colleagues is acting on faith. His learning is not based on his intellect alone—he learns from his gut feelings and the gentle stirrings of his own heart.

Faith is an integrated approach to learning. If one cultivates faith, one learns with both head and heart. Although learning with the head is preferred in our modern educational and organizational systems, the old dictum of learning by heart is of great importance. We see that events that we remember the most from our childhood are the ones that have strong emotions attached to them. We pay attention to our work if our heart is involved in it. Leaders who enable the employees of their organizations to lend their hearts to their jobs promote faith in work. Bill George, chief executive officer of Medtronic, Inc., a multinational biomedical company said the following:

> After all, we spend more time at work than in any other part of our lives. Shouldn't we find significance in our work and the opportunity to use our mind and feeling while appealing to the animating or life giving principles within us? This isn't practicing religion per se but rather devoting our whole being toward a higher purpose in our work.

In organizations we learn from the visible results of our actions. There is a cause and effect relation between the input and output of our work. We introduce a certain process in a manufacturing unit and obtain a certain product. By means of seeing and analyzing the product we verify whether the process was right or not. Our learning follows the natural law of seeing is believing. In the realm of faith, which has its own cause and effect relation, this law of Nature is reversed. Faith operates on the law of believing is seeing. In faith, belief comes first, and results follow. Henry Ford, the doyen of the U.S. automobile industry, rightly said: "If you think you can or you think you can't, you are right."

The Ford Motor Company held on to the belief that every Ford employee should be able to afford a Ford motor car. This belief produced the desired results. The governing law of faith— believing is seeing—operating, not in a vague and indeterminate way but with the same efficacy as any natural law. The problem is not so much with the law but with our lack of total comprehension of it. In medical science, this law is known as the *placebo effect*, which occurs among patients who are cured simply because they believe they will be cured, not because of any medication.

Faith appears as a very abstract concept in the concrete world of organizational life. It is true that faith is not a thing. But faith is not nothing either. *Not a thing* does not mean nothingness. Otherwise, "things" such as love, justice, and compassion would not be felt by us in our organizational lives. Faith is a state of consciousness that, though invisible to our naked eyes, manifests its own laws given the right circumstances.

Total Quality Consciousness The third organizational value that facilitates Self-learning is total quality consciousness. Total quality management has so far looked into the issue of job enrichment by bringing greater refinement to products, systems, and processes on the job. However, it has often neglected the issue of Self-learning through quality consciousness. Quality cir cles are a reality of organizational life all over the world. Now cultivation of quality consciousness has to be brought to the mainstream of management education for quality circles to have an enduring effect. This will result in a spontaneous shift from on-the-job learning to in-the-Self learning.

Quality consciousness comes from the quality of attention we bring to any job in which we are engaged. When our attention to any work is total, we discover a certain magical quality about our work. In age-old artisanry, quality of attention was the most important tool available to artisans. Without mass-producing machines, artisans were required to be extremely diligent and attentive to their crafts. In his book *The Art in a Craft*, Harry Remde wrote the following about the experience of a potter while making a pot:

> Kneading is the potter's first experience of the workable clay. In kneading he becomes familiar with the clay. The motion of his hands and the clay is part of the circular movement that is the essence of the craft. The potter experiences roundness as he kneads. The pot begins early before the clay has had sight of the wheel.
> ... HARRY REMDE, *The Art in a Craft*, 1975

This is what we understand by quality of attention. In total attention, the experience of the work or the production process is fully internalized, so much so that the worker becomes an integral part of the work. The root cause of our alienation from our organizational work today is that we are not as intimately connected to our work as the age-old artisans were to their crafts. As in true artisanry, real learning happens in the process of attention we give to our work. This attention is the essence of learning. The deeper the attention, the greater is the integration among the head, the heart, and the body, and the better is the quality of artisanry. In the words of Remde:

> This is the purpose of the craft, so much being possible in it. The craftsman learns about himself as he works; while he learns, the work exists. He begins to understand, being as dependent on the craft as it is on him. . . . The heart leaps; the head knows; the body performs. These are the three ingredients in a craft.
>
> . . . HARRY REMDE, *The Art in a Craft*, 1975

In organizational work, learning is nothing but realization in action. In the middle of action, we have this sudden insight into something like a flash of lightening. To use the words of J. Krishnamurti: "We say, 'Give me time, let me have more experience, and eventually I will understand.' But have you not noticed that understanding always comes in a flash, never through calculation, through time?" (Krishnamurti, *On Learning and Knowledge*, 1994).

Krishnamurti defined learning as "the active present." Organizational problem solving takes place in the active present, in the middle of action. This active present is the moment of totality of attention. Like the potter on the wheel, who while totally focused on the clay learns through insight, managers learn in the office.

Leaders learn from moment to moment in a Self-referral process. Their learning today is not conditioned by the knowledge of yesterday. They have a freshness and a receptivity and an agility of mind to absorb new learning. While most of us become the prisoners of our experience, leaders stay in touch with the active present. They learn not from memory but from the present moment. Their selves expand in the sheer joy of learning. Their delight in learning bubbles over the confines of their own selves and light up the minds of their co-workers.

True learning is like lighting a lamp. You can light a thousand fires from the same lamp without diminishing the original one. Enlightened leaders are like the first lamp. They generate an inexhaustible source of learning in the organization without in any way diminishing the light that shines through them.

There is a way between voice and presence
where information flows.
In disciplined silence it opens.
With wandering talk it closes.

 . . . JELALUDDIN RUMI (Barks, 1995)

5

Leadership and Communication

SILENCE AS A LANGUAGE

Silence is the womb of language. Silence conceives, prepares, and gives birth to language. A state of silence is not merely an emptiness of sound; it is the fullness of unspoken intelligence. Silence is the pure potentiality of language. Words or sounds are material expressions of this potentiality. Just as the noisy surface of the sea is held together by the vast unruffled depths of water, silence integrates language into meaning and understanding.

Silence is pure consciousness. It is the basic foundation for our understanding of reality. Silence is emergent language. To use the terminology of modern physics, fluctuation of energy and information on the ground of silence creates thoughts. Thoughts are molecules in motion—neuropeptides that flow in a certain pattern through the neural network. When these "thought-molecules" evolve into intelligible rhythms, language is born. If we were to carefully enquire into the process of how language communicates meaning, we would observe that it is not the words themselves that make meaning. Rather, it is in the silent gaps between words that meaning is created.

Communication through language happens as a result of an exchange or transaction of meaning. The law of exchange involves a common value of the objects being exchanged. If we were to exchange dollar with yen, the common value would be purchasing power. Similarly, in an exchange of words, the common value is silence. All words can be reconverted into silence— they emerge from silence and merge into silence.

Freedom of expression has two dimensions. The first is the freedom of speech, and the second is the freedom of silence. Freedom of speech allows us to say what we feel appropriate to talk about. Freedom of silence enables us to explore the deeper voices within us that speak to us without inhibition. Exercising the freedom of speech involves much greater expense of energy than it does to exercise the freedom of silence. In speech, energy fragments into verbal expressions that are nothing but vibrations of sound energy. In silence, energy is integrated into noiseless awareness. If one holds back the urge to talk from time to time, one will experience a surge of energy in the nervous system. Silence is energy conserving. Therefore, a leader consciously cultivates the discipline of silence.

Words take the form of expression, while silence is the ground of experience. When our expression is true to our experience, our communication becomes authentic. Authentic communication is the foundation for effective communication. The root of effective communication can be traced back to silence. The spoken word has two forms, one is the verbal form, which is sound. The other is the preverbal form, which is silence. In the preverbal stage, that is, before a word is articulated through the lips, the word exists as a silent mental vibration. We can almost hear the mental sound if we cultivate our silence. For example, before we pronounce the word *apple*, we have a mental picture of the apple and a corresponding preverbal vibration in our nervous system.

When we speak with conscious control of our words at the pre-verbal stage, our communication is extremely effective.

To understand how words are created from silence, try this experiment in the following sequence:

1. Take any word that you can pronounce comfortably, for example, *leader*, and utter it aloud ten times.
2. Close your lips and utter the same word mentally for a minute. You will experience a distinct vibration of the word *leader* in your mind.
3. Keep your lips closed and close your eyes for a couple of minutes immediately after the second step. Do not think of anything in particular, but pay attention to whatever comes to mind. A very faint vibration of the word *leader* persists somewhere deep in the cellular structure of your mind. If you are alert enough, you will experience how the vibration merges into silence.

All the great spiritual traditions of the world prescribe the discipline of silence as a process of purifying the mind. The Indian sages describe the state of silence as *mouna*. Sri Ramana Maharshi, who practiced silence for several years of his spiritual life, explained the concept of *mouna* in a dialogue with a devotee:

> **The devotee asked:** What is *mouna* [silence]?
> **The Master replied:** *Mouna* is not closing the mouth. It is eternal speech.
> **Devotee:** I do not understand.
> **Master:** That state which transcends speech and thought is *mouna*.
> **Devotee:** How to achieve it?
> **Master:** Hold some concept firmly and trace it back. By such concentration silence results. When practice becomes natural it will end in silence.

The world of Nature is replete with language. Nature communicates, not through verbal expression but through unheard sounds and unseen vibrations. The flower announces its meeting schedule to the bee by means of the subtle vibration of its fragrance. The housefly declares a conference by buzzing its wings. The bat hears vibrations of trees and conducts its business in the silence of the night. Silence is perpetually speaking to us. It is the most effective language known in Nature's organization that enables it to execute its tasks without much resistance. To use Sri Ramana Maharshi's words once again:

> Silence is ever speaking; it is a perennial flow of language; it is interrupted by speaking. These words obstruct that mute language. There is electricity flowing in a wire. With resistance to its passage, it glows as a lamp or revolves as a fan. In the wire it remains as electric energy. Similarly also, silence is the eternal flow of language, obstructed by words.
>   . . . T.M.P. MAHADEVAN, *Talks with Sri Ramana Maharshi,* 1989

Like all languages, silence has a grammar of its own. In human communication silent gestures denote various nouns— names of objects or ideas. Silent postures can convey the sense of specific action or verb. Silent facial expressions can be as descriptive as any adjective. Pauses of silence between words serve as punctuation marks. The classical dance forms of many ancient cultures use the eloquence of silent nuances as a powerful communication tool.

A sensitivity to silence is important in any form of communication. We may compare the state of silence as a blackboard on which we write words. Unless we understand the nature of the board and the quality of its constitution, we cannot write well. Similarly, unless we comprehend our silence, we cannot understand the full range of our ability to communicate.

Another way to describe the function of silence in communication is to use the analogy of instrumental music. A sound made by a stringed musical instrument has two dimensions: a tone and an undertone. A tone is a sound struck by pulling a cord with the finger. A tone is like a verbal sound that has a clearly audible structure that can be interpreted by our ears. But the depth, density, and dimensionality of instrumental music come not from the tone but from the undertone, which is nothing but the receding vibration of sound as it merges into silence. Some music that we like continues to stay with us even after we have stopped hearing it. This is simply because we have paid attention to and grasped the undertone of the music, which we carry with us in the deep structure of our consciousness.

One of the important issues in leadership is the ability to make the right choices. A leader has to make many significant choices in the course of life and work. A wise leader knows that choices are made in the space and time that exist between a certain stimulus and an appropriate response. To use a concrete example, a business leader working for an insurance company is faced with a dilemma in which she has to decide within five minutes whether she should insure a particular business. She has collected all the data relating to this particular business that is possible for her to collect. Yet she is indecisive—she is unable to figure out whether it will be good business or bad business for her company. As she debates over the pros and cons of her two possible choices, time seems to be running out. At this point she sits in silence with her eyes closed and ponders deeply into her thoughts. Then she makes the clinching decision.

Many of us make decisive choices that way. We take stock of our thoughts about possible consequences of the choices we might make. The greater the stakes in the choice, greater is the division of our thoughts into opposite camps. One group of thoughts marshal support for why a certain choice has to be made. Another group of thoughts give us equally convincing reasons why a particular choice should not be made. An uncultivated mind is swayed by one group of thoughts or the other and decides on the spur of the moment. But a mind that has learned the discipline of silence has a look at all the thoughts and after a while quietly slips into the silent gap between thoughts. In this silence the right choice is made with effortless ease.

How does one cultivate the discipline of silence? The following sequence of steps can be extremely helpful in integrating the value of silence into your daily life:

1. Mark a place in one of your rooms as the *silent space*. Make that space as comfortable as you can for you to stay in. Bring in an easy chair or a bed on which you can sit or squat.
2. For fifteen minutes everyday retreat to this space to have an appointment with yourself.
3. Do not talk when you are in the space. Inform the people around you about your intention to be silent so that they understand. It is necessary that you not attempt to attend to phone calls or other distractions once you are in silence.
4. Sit silently with your eyes closed and be aware of the steady traffic of thoughts in your mind, which will become more and more vivid as your silence grows. After you have done this for a while, pay attention to one single thought or idea and trace the thought to its end. Follow the thought until it dissolves in silence in your consciousness.
5. Feel your energy level, composure at work, and the quality of your relationships become enhanced after you go through this exercise for several days.
6. When you are emotionally upset or before you make a significant decision, spend time in your chosen space. This will be of immense help.
7. You may stay in a vacant room where there is complete silence, yet your mind may be full of noise. If, however, you have practiced the art of listening to the noise of chaotic thoughts in your mind, you will learn what real silence is. You can slowly feel how your outer silence leads to an enriching inner silence. Buddha called this the "calmness of the inner sea."

The average human brain can comprehend about five hundred words per minute, but the average human being can speak only about 100 words per minute. This gives us a clue that even the human constitution is designed with a bias toward listening rather than speaking. Silence is the medium of listening. J. Krishnamurti once said that one listens and therefore learns only in a state of attention, a state of silence. Authentic communication can take place where there is silence.

LEADERSHIP AND THE ART OF LISTENING

Mahavira, a contemporary of the Buddha, was an enlightened master who founded the religion known as Jainism. Mahavira talked about the way of the *shravaka*, or the listener, as a path toward enlightenment. Listening was valued in the sacred traditions because it was synonymous with learning. A whole range of sacred literature of India is known as *shrutis*—they were passed on from generation to generation, not as written documents but through listening and memorization. Those who could listen fully became embodiments of the wisdom of the sacred texts.

We learn more deeply through our ears than through our eyes. Our eyes only skim the surface of reality as a succession of forms. The eyes are very linear in their reception of images. When we look at a large gathering in a conference hall, the eyes survey the crowd from front to back, or from left to right. Our eyes can hardly capture the wholeness of the mass of the crowd—they see only fragments of wholeness. The ears, on the other hand, receive sound from a multidimensional perspective—from near and from far, from left as well as from right. While listening we absorb information from multiple directions. That is why when we think deeply about something we tend to close our eyes and listen more through our ears.

The linear logic of communication places listening as the last step in communication. But the fact is that communication actually begins with listening. Even when we speak, we listen to our own voices.

Perhaps we listen first to our unspoken words in our minds before we actually speak them out. Our inner dialogue precedes our outer expression. Deep listening puts us in intimate touch with our inner dialogues. J. Krishnamurti said that when we try to listen we find it extraordinarily difficult, because we are always projecting our opinions and ideas, our prejudices, our background, our inclinations, and our impulses. When they dominate we hardly listen to what is being said because we are flooded with our inner turmoil.

When leaders listen, they first pay attention to their inner impulses. By doing so they establish communication with their own selves. They bring to the light of consciousness the background noise of their own voices. Once this noise has settled down, true listening begins. Otherwise, the leader imposes his own voice on the voice of the person to whom he is listening. This distorts his reception of messages from others. The process of inner listening is like fine tuning your inner radio to a specific frequency to clear out the internal noise so that you can hear the news clearly.

Listening, like language, has more than one dimension. First, there is the *dimension of the factual*. At this level language is merely a statement of fact. For example, when someone informs us that it rained last weekend or that a company has increased its profits by ten percent, we listen to statements of facts. Listening to such facts does not require much subtlety, anyone with a certain amount of attention can do that.

The second dimension of language is the *dimension of the intentional*. At this level one has to listen to the more subtle intent behind what a speaker says. When a boss tells a subordinate, "I appreciate your coming to the office on time today," she is conveying a different message from what the mere words would communicate. The subordinate who listens well reads the message as, "I do not appreciate your coming late to the office every other day." Intentional listening requires greater attention and energy on the part of the listener.

The third and the most subtle dimension of language is the *transformational dimension*. Language has a certain alchemy that can transform the heart and mind of the listener. This transformation comes about in the listener through a process known as *empathy*. When listening is very deep, the listener is in touch with the spirit behind the speaker's words. He listens with his heart behind his ears. The focus of the listener is not merely on the words or the intention behind them but on the raw energy of the words. Those who have had the good fortune to listen to the "dream" speech of Martin Luther King, Jr., would certainly have experienced the transformational aspect of listening.

Conscious leaders have the ability to listen simultaneously to three dimensions of language—the factual, the intentional, and the transformational. They pick up factual details with the precision of a scientist; gain insight into the intention of the speaker with the imagination of a poet, and are willing to be transformed by what they hear with the zeal of a pilgrim. Ultimately, listening is not merely about gathering information but is about transformation of this information into intelligence. Deep listening facilitates the flow of intelligence in communication by removing the physical, physiologic, and mental barriers that separate the speaker from the listener.

Rumi (Barks, 1995) said the following:

A tongue has one customer, the ear.

The relation between the tongue and the ear is not like a mechanical relation between one organ of the body and another. It is not as though the tongue pours out information and the ear receives it. The relation is one of unity and dynamic interdependence. The roles of the tongue and the ear are interchangeable. Sometimes the ear speaks and the tongue silently listens. The ear is a creative speaker; it listens to sound and makes meaning from it and like a skilled interpreter conveys the correct meaning. All this while, the tongue remains silent, for if it did not, it would have interrupted the ear and distorted understanding. Leaders know that the purpose of listening is to create not eloquence but understanding. They follow Shakespeare's dictum: "Give every man thy ear, but few thy voice" (*Hamlet*, Act I, scene iii).

WORDS: HOW THEY SHAPE OUR WORLD

> "When *I* use a word," Humpty Dumpty said, in a rather scornful tone, "it means just what I choose it to mean—neither more nor less."
>
> "The question is," said Alice, "whether you *can* make words mean so many different things."
>
> . . . Lewis Carroll, *Through the Looking-Glass*, 1872

The word is not a human invention. Nor is it a mere tool of communication; it is infinitely more. It does not merely convey an empty sound or a rational idea devoid of power. The word has many forms: it has a material aspect, a meaning, a message, a visible structure, and a certain quality of vibration. To enter the most intimate structure of a word, one has to participate in the very process or act by which the word comes into existence. The word is both a material creation of reality and the invisible intelligence that creates reality.

All words exist in seed form as sound. In this form the word is a conscious but undifferentiated principle. Then the sound becomes differentiated in the mind and takes the form of a thought. Finally it becomes articulate speech as it passes through different organs of articulation such as the larynx, tongue, palate, teeth, and lips.

In the seed form, the word as sound is nothing but conscious energy. At this stage the word does not acquire audibility or amplitude and is merely an intention. Under the impulse of perception, this conscious energy of intention creates a nervous tension in the mind that seeks release through speech.

So we see that the genesis of a word is a conscious intention that resides in the ground of undifferentiated sound. To put it in another perspective, a word evolves from the unified field of natural intelligence. To illustrate this, let us take the example of two English words—*rock* and *flower*. Even to a person who has not learned English, the sound of the word *rock* would convey something hard and heavy, whereas with the word *flower* one would experience something soft and delicate. Besides denoting natural objects, these words also have psychological nuances. For example, *rock* can denote someone with a strong and inflexible temperament. From the experiential point of view, words cannot be said to be the outcome of human organization. Rather, they evolve in the mindscape of human beings from the landscape of the ineffable intelligence of Nature.

Words are the makers of the material reality of our world. Without words, it is impossible to imagine the highly specialized organizations of today. Words such as *capital*, *property*, *target*, *market*, *management*, *customers*, and *communication* constitute what we may call the speaking structure of our organization. If we were to trace the origin of some of these words, we would be surprised to find that they come not so much from the mind of humans as they do from the evocative field of Nature. In the preindustrial age, the word *capital* meant wealth in terms of cattle. In those days cattle was an important factor in production and a bounty of Nature. Similarly, the word *property* came from the Latin word *proprius*, which means "one's own nature." Thus from the original meaning of "natural quality," the notion of property acquired a more material meaning, that is, "real estate to which a person has exclusive legal rights."

Natural forms and phenomena create the deep structure of words. In the course of civilization such natural words acquire material forms that are almost divorced from their source. The word *trade* now means to do business. Originally this word meant a recurring habit or manner in life or a path traversed as in "treading a path." From this it acquired the restricted meaning of work or a profession. Now a trader is one who sells commodities. Similarly, *shop* meant "a place for cattle to stay," as in Anglo-Saxon *scypen*, or a "cart-house," as in German *schuppen*. The English word *measure* originates in the ancient Sanskrit expression *maya*, which means an illusion of Nature. The conception of *maya* arose from the understanding of the ancient Indian civilization that all measurements show us only fragmentary surfaces of the reality of Nature and therefore cannot be fully relied upon.

All of our sacred literature tells us that a word is a conscious vehicle between things and thoughts. In the Book of Genesis we read: "And God said, Let there be light: and there was light" (I:1–3).

The Vedas tell us: ". . . by that word of his, by that Self, he created all this, whatever there is." The Holy Qur'an similarly says: "Our only word to a thing, when we desire it, it is to say to it Be! and it is." At the stage of its conception, the word is a primal energy of Nature, a pure vibration of immense potential. Nature also thinks, not through verbal language as we do, but through the vibration of sound.

The difference between a tree and a stone is merely a qualitative difference in the vibration of the same atoms. The word stands as a bridge between the vibration of the natural world, which is things, and the vibration of the mental world, which is thoughts. The process of conversion of thoughts to things and vice versa happens through the word. The Gospel of John says about this process: "In the beginning was the Word. . . . The Word was made flesh" (I:1,14).

The mechanics of creation of meaning out of sound or word has remained a mystery to modern scientists. The notion that language is purely a material expression devoid of consciousness is no longer scientifically tenable. Walt Whitman's assertion that "All words are spiritual—nothing is more spiritual than words" may really be the most scientific truth about the nature and origin of language. In our own lives we must have experienced the influence that some words wield over us. Words like *love* and *power* can trigger an experience of great magnitude in our consciousness.

The outer structures of words have by themselves no meaning. It is only the true experience of the inner consciousness of words that fills them with meaning. The potential of a piece of elastic is not realized until you are willing to stretch it. The meanings of words can be realized only when you allow the word to stretch itself in your consciousness.

Modern organizations have stripped words out of their conscious contents and have reduced them to items of commerce. Kathleen Raine, a contemporary British writer, said in an interview in *Parabola* magazine: "You see, you can either fill words with meaning or you can empty meanings out of words. We're living in a linguistically reductionist society. Everything means less and less" (*Parabola*, August, 1983).

Even in the middle of the information explosion that has gripped modern organizations, we seem to be saying more and meaning less. We have reduced the whole conception of the joy and richness of work to a single word: *pay*. We wish our colleagues, "Good morning!" matter of factly without even bothering to pause to let the feeling of goodness come through our voice. By robbing our words of meanings we have de-meaned our life and work.

Leaders bring to their words a certain consciousness of the spirit of the words. Before leaders tell you, "Good morning," they experience the goodness of the morning in themselves. They shake your hand, look straight into your eyes, take a deep breath, bring their attention to the words that come from the depth of their hearts and say, "Good Morning, Jean." You do not so much hear the words as you hear the conviction in the leader's voice and feel the energy of her words. This is the secret of high-touch leadership.

PROBLEM SOLVING: LIVING IN QUESTIONS

Marvin Minsky, a leader in the world of artificial intelligence, says that you do not understand anything until you learn it more than one way. Organizational problem solving involves the ability to look at a single problem from multidimensional perspectives. For example, a problem relating to the quality of a certain product of an organization has to be looked at from the points of view of various segments of the organization: production, marketing, manufacturing, and of course, the customer. Leaders, who often take on the role of problem solver, integrate the multiple points of views in their organization in their endeavors to arrive at a decisive solution.

To integrate the many ways of looking at a problem, the leader has to live in questions. A leader who believes in giving quick-fix answers is, more often than not, compounding the problem. The quick-fix solution itself multiplies the problem into two parts. One part can be remedied with a clean-up operation, and the other part can be pushed under the carpet temporarily. That which is pushed under the carpet, however, triggers a new set of problems the magnitude of which may be incalculable. To solve the "problem" of a crying child, a certain mother provides a quick-fix solution: give the child whatever he wants. This pacifies the child momentarily, and the crying stops. A new problem begins with this kind of a solution—the child does not learn the discipline of patience. This new problem is compounded as the child grows in years to have an abusive and intemperate personality.

So the conscious leader, like the wise mother, learns to live in questions rather than in immediate answers. The mother asks herself: Why does the child cry so much? Does she want more candy or more attention? Is she feeling lonely? Do I need to give her more time? Perhaps she is physically not well. With this kind of relentless questioning, the mother goes nearer to an enduring solution.

In our conventional educational systems, questions are considered to be incomplete states of awareness. Naturally, one is programmed in such a system to find answers quickly. A questioning mind is not valued in societies, whereas ready-made answers are desperately sought. Organizations that are perpetually in a hurry to search for answers quickly forget to ask the right questions. General Motors had a large market share of automobiles when cars were bought primarily as status symbols. The company had found a ready answer to grab market share:

people buy cars for style and not for quality. They stopped asking questions about quality and price of cars because they were concerned only with style. Soon the Japanese carmakers entered the market with the right question: Can we make cars that have both quality and style? The Japanese also asked: Does high quality necessarily mean high price? They were thus getting closer to the secret of their success in the automobile market: it is possible to provide stylish cars with high quality and lower price.

If a question is held long enough in the consciousness of the questioner, this very act brings the questioner to a heightened state of awareness. A question is nothing but concentration of energy on an aspect of our reality that appears foggy to us. The more intense the questioning, the greater is the concentration of energy on the fogginess of the reality. A state comes when the question has persisted long enough for the accumulated energy to transform itself into a higher level of awareness. In this awareness the fogginess around the problem is dispelled. When we encounter a dark room, we take out a match and strike hard on the surface of the matchbox. At first strike there is no light. So we strike a second time, and only a flicker of light comes and dies out. So we strike again and again until we have a flash of light and a clear flame. This happens because the energy at the tip of the match has reached a flash point. Thus we can illuminate the dark room.

Socrates said that answers are often ignorance mistaking itself for knowledge. Answers are deadends. They are like blind alleys for a questioning mind. Answers that are shallow and symptomatic block the evolution of knowledge. Ready answers come from our fear of the unknown. They are our search for security in time-tested and habitual patterns of behavior and action. A question is alive with energy. If one asks the right question, no answer is needed. The question itself dissolves in the light of consciousness.

A problem arises only when the wholeness of our life is seen in parts. Disintegration of life is the root of any problem. All environmental problems are the consequence of the disintegration between our inner environment with our outer environment. We see this disintegration even in our organizational life when there is a split between our ultimate goals and immediate tasks, between our principles and practices, and between our heads and hearts. By treating outer symptoms instead of inner causes we continue to be a part of the problem. Solutions emerging from our fragmented perspectives become problems by themselves. We are like blind persons perpetually complaining about the darkness in the outer world.

In organizations, we rush to solve problems without stopping to ask what created the problem in the first place. While trying to find solutions in our present system, we become trapped by the rules of the existing system. We do not bother to look at our accustomed ways of looking and thinking. We do not control our thoughts. Our thoughts control us. They condition the very way we negotiate problems.

Leadership is a quest and not a fixed target. A leader lives in questions and not in answers. The Brihadaranyaka Upanishad describes the quest of a leader in an elegant phrase: *neti neti charaibeti*, not here, not here, move on. This relentless movement of the leader is a movement in the realm of consciousness. While making the journey leaders discover that today's problem is a result of yesterday's solution. The response to this discovery is greater receptivity and the beginning of a dialogue with themselves. In a dialogue, there is no final solution; there is only the flow of intelligence through the recesses of the mind. When intelligence flows, a problem need not be solved—it simply dissolves by itself.

COMMUNICATION: A TRYST WITH TRUTH

Mark Reuben, a successful chief executive officer of Colgate Palmolive told *Fortune* magazine recently that "You've got to be honest and straightforward: what you tell the outside world has to be the same thing you tell your senior people, and the same thing you tell your factory workers." While this may sound like a cliché, all leaders realize in the short or the long run that the foundation of effective communication is authentic communication.

A wise Indian sage put it this way: "May my word be firmly established in my mind. May my mind be firmly established in my word." Authentic communication demands oneness of content and intent, synchronicity of speech and thought, and a simultaneous awareness of both sound and silence. The content of our communication comes from *what* we say, and the intent comes from *why* we say it. Oneness of what and why demands a certain quality of consciousness. Speakers need to be in touch with the ulterior motives that propel their speech. They need to be certain that the internal dialogue in their minds does not come in the way of what they actually say.

Synchronicity in our internal dialogue and external communication means that we are in touch with our spontaneity. The energy of thoughts and the energy of speech come together in this synchronicity. Speech becomes free flowing like the course of a river from which all obstacles have been removed. Such a speech carries with it the power of dynamism. Communication that originates from the core of the Self has an irresistible natural power like that of heat and light.

Rajat Gupta, the first non-American leader of the global consulting firm McKinsey and Company is an effective communicator. One of his colleagues says about his leadership style: "Gupta gets more done by talking less than anyone I know." Effective communication has a certain correlation with silence and economy of speech. The leader speaks only to facilitate understanding. Sometimes language can be a barrier to understanding. If language confuses rather than facilitates understanding, it is wise to clear the clutter of words through silence.

Leadership communication is a tryst with truth. By truth I mean not merely an absence of lies but an active pursuit of what is real in the ultimate sense. Gandhi said: "Truth is my God." His experiment with truth was nothing but pursuing with uncompromising zeal the ultimate natural law that animates all form and phenomena. At the end of his journey, Gandhi discovered that there is no way to find truth except the way of nonviolence. Every leader discovers his or her way of seeking out truth. But the ultimate result is the same: a life that communicates the power and passion of authentic living. It is only then the leader can say, "My life is my message."

The credibility of a leader communicates more eloquently than his or her words. Credibility comes from character. I define character as consistency in conduct. If a leader demonstrates such consistency in the smallest of actions, he or she is likely to demonstrate this consistency in larger actions. Credibility of large magnitude comes from credibility in small actions. One of the allies of credibility is transparency of action. Lack of transparency leads to lack of trust, and this lowers the credibility of the leader. Gandhi called secrecy the enemy of credibility. In secrecy we merely withhold ourselves. We create an artificial barrier between our inner nature and outer nature. The power of our communication is reduced in proportion to the extent a secret barrier exists within us.

In the final analysis, character in communication comes when we say only what we believe can be realized. This means we need to learn the discipline of not indulging in speaking thoughtlessly. This also means that we are neither too high in praise nor too low in blaming someone. We do not give false encouragement to our subordinates, nor do we plunge them into despair with our angry outbursts. Leaders learn to communicate with a consciousness that their words are capable of changing the destinies of the people with whom they are communicating. They therefore believe the following wise maxim:

> Sow a thought, and you reap an act;
> Sow an act, and you reap a habit;
> Sow a habit, and you reap a character;
> Sow a character, and you reap a destiny.
>
> . . . ANONYMOUS, QUOTED BY
> SAMUEL SMILES, *Life and Labor*, 1887

Try not to become a man of success but rather try to become a
man of value.

. . . ALBERT EINSTEIN

6

*Leadership
and Human Values*

TRADITION AND TRANSFORMATION:
FROM METAPHOR TO METAMORPHOSIS

Tradition, like statistics, has a way of discovering reality. In statistics, we all know that the larger the sample size, that is, the
greater the spread of data collected, the closer is the sample to
reality. In the context of various traditions, the deeper a tradition
goes in time, the greater is the chance that it is telling you deeper
truths about the realities of human existence. Some of the basic
human values, such as love, compassion, and freedom, that the
sacred traditions have upheld for ages are perhaps the most
enduring elements of human organizations.

Traditions are built and held together by some values that
are like social contracts. These values are not as tangible as the
constitution of a country; they are codified in human behavior
and rituals and are passed on from generation to generation. They
also constitute the deeper structures of organizational realities of
specific cultures. If you ask a manager of a corporation in the

United States, "What is your profession?" you are likely to hear a response such as "I am a marketing manager" or "software engineer" or some such response related to professional qualification. The same question when asked of a Japanese manager would yield a response such as "I work for Sony" or "I am an employee of Toyota." Whereas one culture values individuality, the other values community.

The process of modernization sometimes brings about modification in culture-specific values. For example, in traditional Indian culture, the son was identified with the father's profession. In contemporary India, however, this value has weakened considerably. In Asian societies in which "women should not go out to work" was a strongly held value, we are witnessing increasing "womanization" of the workforce. But tradition goes much deeper than societal values. Traditions evolve from lived experiences of individuals about certain truths of life—how to conduct oneself in one's own life in order to function effectively and harmoniously. These truths are then accepted and codified as values, norms, and rituals by members of a society.

Tradition establishes the possibility of the continuance of the experience of a certain community of individuals in larger spans of time and space through the practice of certain values. By themselves these values and rituals have only symbolic significance. Unless they are lived and experienced by individuals themselves, they serve little purpose. It is not enough to know intellectually about the Christian tradition or the Buddhist tradition or the Indian tradition. It is easy to be a Christian by subscribing to a certain church. But the real experience of the Christian tradition comes when we try to live a life as Christ did. It is easy to become a Buddhist but not so easy to be a Buddha. Traditions are like footprints on the sands of time. They show you the way a leader has traveled before you, that is all. If you want to find out what the leaders, did you have to travel on your own. The Zen master Basho said: "Do not seek to follow in the footsteps of the wise; seek what they sought."

Traditions undergo change not because the truths they are upholding are not valid any more. Human beings, by nature, are creative beings. They are always looking for new ways of arriving at the same goal. Traditions do not transform by themselves either. It is only the people who undergo transformation. Traditions are simply metaphors that suggest the possibility of a human metamorphosis.

To be able to bring about human transformation, all traditions have to be made contemporary. They have to be lived over and over again before their value begins to unfold. In the absence of lived experience, traditions are reduced to empty shells of mindless rules. Trying to recapture great truths with a network of moral and organizational rules alone is as futile as trying to hold water in a fishing net. Very often, truth experienced by a leader through a certain tradition becomes lost in the process of elaborate organization. There is an amusing story about a man who climbs to the top of a mountain and discovers truth:

> *Some followers of the devil who came to know about this extraordinary man were horrified. They sensed that this man would be a threat to the devil's kingdom. They ran to the devil and reported the incident. The devil listened to them calmly and said, "Don't worry, let him come down from the mountain; all I need to do is to tempt him to organize truth."*

When organizations become rigid, they merely ritualize tradition; when they are dynamic they enliven tradition to evolve into newer forms and capacities.

Organizations are complex structures capable of dynamism in response to changes in the environment. Every organizational structure, however, needs a certain amount of stability provided by tradition to assimilate change. The human body is a complex organization that is undergoing change every moment. But there is the much needed stability in the human constitution—the genetic code for example, which provides the necessary traditional foundation for the body's dynamism. In the case of organizations, this stability comes from the core values and the myths and stories about the organization that are passed from one generation of employees to another.

Leaders transform organizations not by imitating other successful organizations but by looking deeply within the tradition of their own organizations. They listen to the voices of the people who have been there for some time, the success stories they tell, the reasons they ascribe to failures, the aspirations they articulate, and the values that they cherish. Leaders simply energize and facilitate the spontaneous flowering of indigenous ideas within the organization. They constitute the invisible tradition of the organization. They are indeed the symbolic seeds for inside-out transformation of the organization—metaphors that bring about metamorphosis.

HUMAN VALUES: THE DEEP STRUCTURE OF LEADERSHIP

"We exist to provide value to our customers—to make their lives better via lower prices and greater selection; all else is secondary." This is the gospel of a leading corporation, Wal-Mart. It is a values statement that characterize what may be described as the Wal-Mart tradition. Its stated values give the company a continuity in time and define the rationale for its continuous existence. Can you imagine any organization whose members do not want continuity of its life? It is the deep-seated life instinct of an organization that impels its members to search for life-affirming values.

In organizations there are two types of leaders: the first follow the path of desire, and the second follow the path of the desirable. As a wit remarked, the second type serve as the pillars of an organization, while the first type serve as caterpillars. Human values pave the path of the desirable. What then are human values? How are they different from any other kind of value, such as commercial value, scientific value, or aesthetic value? First of all, human values are the deep structure of human consciousness that determine all other kinds of values— scientific, commercial, and artistic.

Take the example of Tata Iron and Steel Company (TISCO), India's largest private-sector company to manufacture steel. TISCO describes itself in the following words: "We also make steel." The commercial value of TISCO in making profits is seen by the company as a consequence of its embracing a much broader human value. Its commercial value lies in asset building while the human value lies in institution building. The truth that a core human value can lead to commercial value is established by the continuous success of TISCO as one of India's most valuable companies.

Even scientific value is a function of broader human value. Scientists acknowledge today that their basic assumptions about reality determine what they are out to observe in the laboratories. When we look at the evolution of two distinct forms of medical sciences—modern medicine of the last few centuries and traditional herbal medicine—we see how the basic human values behind each of these two forms of medicine have determined the course of their history. Modern medicine is based on the basic premise of curing disease through investigation and analysis. Traditional forms of medicine, such as *ayurveda*, are based on creating health by restoring the human being's lost harmony with Nature. The first type focuses on disease, and the second focuses on health—physical, mental and spiritual. One goes to a doctor today to know the secret of disease; but does anyone ask the doctor: "Please, tell me the secret of my health?"

Human values are the invisible roots of organizational values. They determine the rationale for which an organization exists. Human values are distinct from commercial values in that they are not so much guided by the will to get as they are by the will to give. Sony wants its employees "to experience the sheer joy that comes from the advancement, application, and innovation of technology that benefits the general public." Sony thrives on the will to give its customers joy and happiness. Its will to get a larger market share for itself is subordinated to larger human values.

The task of a leader in an organization is to nurture the roots of organizational values, which consist of nothing but a basic human aspiration—the will to give. Human values come from our deeper state of being, where we are not asking, "What is there in it for me?" Rather, in our very depths we humans are saying, "What can I contribute? How can I share myself with others? What can I leave behind for posterity?" Each one of us in an organization is looking for the freedom to be a true self and for the freedom to serve to the best of our capacity. Our deepest aspirations are not quite met in wanting more and more and more for ourselves but in wanting to give more of ourselves—in wanting to be larger than life. A leader is a projection of this common aspiration.

In a survey conducted in twelve Indian organizations of one thousand managers spread throughout the country, researchers asked: What are some of the qualities that you look for in a leader? The respondents gave the following as the top five attributes of a good leader:

1. Dynamism
2. Inspiring character
3. Vision
4. Ethical values
5. Spiritual strength

It was evident from the responses that Indian managers were defining leadership from the deeper perspective of core human values and not as a function of superficial skills. The core leadership values of character, spiritual strength, and vision remain the cornerstone of the highest aspirations of practicing managers. The study further revealed a cultural congruence within the Indian tradition that prompted managers from different parts of the country to subscribe to the same set of values despite differences in age, sex, language, and qualifications.

In a 1993 article in *Time* magazine, James Walsh examined how Confucian societies in Asia, such as those of Singapore and Taiwan, are challenging western liberalism with their own ideas of democratic values. Confucian ethos is a legacy of a broad stream of ancient sages, including Lao-tzu. This ethos emphasizes the following human values: communitarian standards, deference to elders and authority, and civic responsibilities in place of civil rights. The Confucian values system upholds the tradition of hierarchy and duties implicit in the social structure and psychological theory of most Eastern cultures. These cultures demonstrate their sacred deference to the leader, whom Confucius compares with the wind: "The grass must bend when the wind blows over it."

The capacity of leadership in Confucian democracies is determined by a deeply held human value: the ability to bring harmony in human relationships. Confucianism emphasizes the principle of harmony in all aspects of personal, social, and organizational relationships. Mencius, an ancient scholar of the Confucian school spoke of five basic harmonies:

> . . . between father and son, there should be affection; between ruler and minister, there should be righteousness; between husband and wife, there should be attention to their separate functions; between old and young, there should be a proper order, and between friends, there should be faithfulness.
>
> . . . Mencius, in Wing-sit Chan,
> *A Source Book in Chinese Philosophy,* 1963

In modern Taiwan, the age-old human value of harmony still serves as the core leadership principle in politics and business. In the words of Yao Chia-wen, a leader of Taiwan's democratic political party: "Harmony is more important in our society, so people do not put so much value on equality or personal freedom" (*Time*, June 14, 1993).

HIERARCHY AND THE NEW ORDER IN ORGANIZATIONS

Hierarchy is a dirty word in contemporary business. Hierarchical organizations, which still persist in most parts of the world, are looked down upon as high-fat, low-calorie, and low-energy companies. The in-thing today is a network organization in which information flows from one part to another like a flit-footed ballerina. The visual metaphors are too compelling to ignore. It does seem as though organizational hierarchies, like the dinosaur, are destined to die an evolutionary death. However, in hastening the dissolution of hierarchies in contemporary organizations, there is a pervasive lack of understanding of the true nature of hierarchy and its implication for human development.

One of the most misconceived notions about hierarchy is that it exists only in the physical structuring of an organization. In the process we ignore the evidences of hierarchies in the psychological organization of human beings. In contemporary organizations one hears about fast-track employees, implying that there is a hierarchical presence of slow-track workers. There are key-performance areas, which means there are areas in which performance may be kept at a relatively low key. In modern parlance there may be diminishing evidence of vertical, pyramid-like sizes of organizations, but there is certainly more and more down-sizing, whereby there exists an invisible hierarchy of those who can survive and those who cannot.

In Nature hierarchies exist as vividly as the force of gravity. Water flows from a higher plane to a lower plane. Silver has higher potential than lead, so electricity flows from a silver rod to a lead rod when they are dipped in a conducting solution. The entire food chain is a horrid hierarchy of higher life forms eating lower ones. Hierarchies in Nature appear as an ordering of relationships, the basic purpose of which is to facilitate the flow of energy.

The evolution of human beings represents a progress of human potential. The species we know as *Homo sapiens* is not the final outcome of Nature's evolutionary urge. The human being we know today is only a transitional state and not a stable destination. In other words, human evolution is an evolution of consciousness. In the context of our modern organizations, such an evolution of consciousness is taking place, and hierarchies are being redefined.

What we are witnessing in network organizations is not abolishing of hierarchies but reworking of the existing hierarchies in different dimensions. Organizations are composed of structures of multiple dimensions. We are accustomed to seeing only a linear dimension of hierarchy—the physical structure of the organization described with an organizational chart in the form of a ladder or pyramid. But other dimensions exist simultaneously with functional hierarchies; these are hierarchies of actual responsibilities, which is not the same as hierarchies of designation. There are also hierarchies of age, hierarchies of knowledge and information, and hierarchies of emotional stability. All these multiple structures of hierarchies fuse together in the complex structure of relationships through which organizations actually function. Network organizations of today are nothing but the discovery of this relational dimension of organization. They do not make functional hierarchies redundant; they only allow the potential of many other hierarchies to be unlocked in a larger web of relationships.

No relationship can exist without a difference in potential. Whether it is a relationship between two metals, between members of a family, or in the larger contexts of organization. The preconditions for any relationship are not only diversity but also a difference in potential. In Japanese organizations, the relationship of *sempai-kohai* is a relationship of the elder brother with the younger brother. There is difference of perspective in this relationship. The elder brother is not necessarily better than the younger brother in ability, but he is more responsible because he is higher in age. The privilege of being the elder entails greater authority but also more responsibility. He may demand obedience, but he also has to be illustrious. The younger brother treats the elder with respect. This respect is nothing but the emotional acknowledgment of the fact that the younger must rise to the higher potential of the elder.

In the more intimate relationship that exists within one's self, there is an internal yardstick of values by which we evaluate our thoughts and actions. This qualitative interpretation of our own progress as human beings is what provides the motivational energy for our evolution as human beings. Leadership in organizations is an onward movement toward a higher state of consciousness. This higher state is not something that is opposed to something lower. *Higher state* means a state that can encompass the lower and at the same time provide the impetus for the lower to rise to the dimension of the higher.

Conscious leaders understand the value of hierarchy as a deeper form of democracy. For them, people and things do not remain static as higher or lower. The relationship between them evolves with the evolution of consciousness. The common value between the higher and the lower is this dynamic relationship. The leader realizes that being great requires just as much potential and perseverance as being humble. Golda Meir once said to an acquaintance: "Don't be so humble. You're not that great." Conscious leaders do not talk about nonexistence of hierarchies. Rather, they gain insight into the everchanging kaleidoscope of hierarchies that mix and merge into the vast unity of pure consciousness. They looks at human-made and natural hierarchies with a fresh perspective. They realize like the Zen master that hierarchies are relative, what is absolute is pure consciousness:

> Before enlightenment mountains are mountains and waters
>   are waters;
> During enlightenment, mountains are no longer mountains
>   and waters no longer waters;
> After enlightenment, mountains are once again mountains
>   and waters once again waters.

A leader understands the organization of all form and phenomena of Nature as an interdependent play of position and perspective. Hierarchies in human organizations are just that—an amalgam of position and perspective. This is what constitutes the ground of relationships within the organization. The superior positions of leaders only gives them greater perspective. Truly conscious leaders use position not to get greater perquisite but to gain better perspective of organizational reality.

SHARED VALUES: LEADERSHIP AS RELATIONSHIP

The ultimate value of leadership is not positional but is relational. Russi Mody, India's most charismatic corporate leader, believes that the leader's main source of strength lies in human relationships. In an address to my MBA students he said:

> The Bible is the only book on modern management that I have read. The Bible contains the wisdom of the Ten Commandments. Two of the commandments are: A. Do unto others as you would have them do unto you. B. Love thy neighbor as thyself. . . . It is a philosophy on which good industrial relations can be built, good personnel management can be practiced and excellent human relations developed.

The essence of human relationships is that one does not view the other person as an object from the outside. Rather, one experiences within one's self what the other person is experiencing. This is true empathy. The Sanskrit expression for this is *Tat twam asi*, which literally means, "I am You." When one is in a deep relationship, the barrier between *I* and *You* is bridged by an inexplicable communion of spirit. The mother feels this communion with her child, the lover feels it with his beloved, the devotee feels it with the divine, and the leader feels it with the led. In this communion there is total abandonment of the self, and in this communion alone true communication takes place.

Lonnie Barbach in an article in the *Chicago Tribune* wrote the following:

> When you look at relationships that make it, the people are good friends and treat each other with respect, they have shared values and they trust one another. Trust is the foundation. Without it you don't feel safe. If you don't feel safe, you can't be vulnerable. If you are not vulnerable, you can't be intimate.

Intimacy in a relationship comes from self-abandonment. It is the act of laying down the defenses of our insecure selves, of being open to scrutiny. When we have nothing to defend, we become truly invincible. Gandhi's philosophy of nonviolence was a philosophy of defenselessness. By being totally vulnerable, Gandhi could disarm the most formidable of opponents. As Gandhi himself said, "It is to me a matter of perennial satisfaction that I retain generally the affection and the trust of those whose principles and policies I oppose" (Fischer, 1962).

In building relationships within an organization, leaders do not necessarily have to bring everyone to their points of view. This is not possible in large organizations, in which there are bound to be disagreements and dissenting voices. If leaders try to crush any opposition to their views or actions, they only end up creating walls of resistance before their adversaries. By being defenseless and transparent, they disarm their opponents, who have nothing to attack. Gandhi overcame his opponents by appealing to and arousing what he called the *soul-force* in them. When leaders operate from a higher reference point of conduct and action, they can relate even to those who stand against them.

Max DePree said, "You have to look at leadership through the eyes of the follower." Leaders have the unenviable task of having to accommodate a thousand minds in the pursuit of an organizational goal. How do they do that? Swami Vivekanada, a great institutional builder himself, said that to do this a leader has to be "a servant of servants." Conscious leaders lead from behind. By choosing to serve they eliminate partiality, prejudice, and power motives from the repertoire of their actions. Thus they gain the moral mandate to lead, though they have come only to serve.

LEADERSHIP MOTIVATION: THE LAW OF GIVING

"Many times a day I realize how much my own inner and outer life is built on the labors of other men, both living and dead, and how earnestly I must exert myself in order to give in return as much as I have received." These are not the words of a saint but of a scientist—Albert Einstein, whose life was a saga of a search for eternal truths of life. A life of giving is a life of self-expansion. In giving, the self becomes an expression of Nature's eternal cycle of creation, preservation, and transformation. Giving is the creative process of transformation of self to Self. In giving, one's self becomes part of the perennial flow of energy in the cosmos. To give is to grow.

The inspiration to give comes spontaneously to a leader. A conscious leader understands the paradox of Nature in which the law of giving functions in reverse direction to the law of grabbing. As one grabs more money, power, and status one accumulates. As one hoards what one has accumulated, one grows poorer and poorer. This poverty is the outcome of the limiting law of material wealth. All material wealth diminishes in time and in unfavorable circumstances. The grabbing mind is forever insecure that its wealth will be taken away by someone else. A large part of the energy of this mind is wasted in its anxiety to hold on to what it has got. This insecurity is the price of poverty consciousness.

Nature turns this principle around in the law of giving. Giving is building capacity for accommodating not for accumulating. As we build capacity to accommodate the other, we shift our limited energy toward generating more and producing more. In short, by giving we promote our selves to wealth consciousness. The more we empty the air from a room, the more air comes in. If we had closed the room from all sides, air may have accumulated for some time. But that air would soon become stale, and we would perish in it.

Taoism describes this process of giving through the symbolic expression of emptiness. The capacity of a clay pot depends on the emptiness of space it has and not so much on the material of the container. What exists in material form serves for possession and that which does not exist in material form but in terms of space or capacity serves for effectiveness. Therefore, says Lao-tzu:

> The Man of Calling does not heap up possessions.
> The more he does for others,
> The more he possesses.
> The more he gives to others,
> The more he has.
>
> *. . . Tao Te Ching*

When the flower blooms, bees fly in without invitation. Leaders learn through experience that the law of giving results in the flowering of a new state of consciousness. This state of consciousness activates the affluence or the "flowing in" of material Nature's bounties. Consciousness, which is spiritual affluence, is the primal cause and material affluence is the consequence. Between the cause and consequence, the mechanics of the law of giving operate. Wealth comes to the spiritually affluent person as spontaneously as bees come to a flower and as effortlessly as air fills an empty room.

Clinging to possessions results in the burden of accumulation. On the contrary, affluence is the fullness of being that comes from giving. "Give what you have to give. It will come back to you. . . . But do not think of that now . . . it will come back to you multiplied a thousand fold," said Swami Vivekananda. When we give from a sense of abundance, we always find ourselves in abundance. This is an infallible law of Nature.

In giving with joy, leaders enact the inviolable law of Nature's kingdom. They realize that Nature will eventually take away what is not given. The body, mind, power, and privilege and all that is held dear will ebb away with the tide of time. The hairs will turn gray, the skin will wrinkle, the eyes will fail, and intellect will be dulled. What will remain in circulation even when we are not around are the intangible things we gave away—the little acts of love, the gifts of service, companionship, and compassion. Kahlil Gibran wrote the following:

> There are those who give little of the much which they have—
> and they give it for recognition and their hidden desire makes
> their gifts unwholesome.
>
> And there are those who have little and give it all.
>
> These are the believers in life and the bounty of life, and their
> coffer is never empty.
>
> There are those who give with joy, and that joy is their
> reward.
>
> And there are those who give with pain, and that pain is their
> baptism.
>
> And there are those who give and know not pain in giving,
> nor do they seek joy, nor give with mindfulness of virtue; . . .
>
> It is well to give when asked, but it is better to give unasked,
> through understanding; . . .
>
> You often say, "I would give, but only to the deserving."

The trees in your orchard say not so, nor the flocks in your pasture.
They give that they may live, for to withhold is to perish.

. . . Kahlil Gibran, *The Prophet*, 1923

Self-managed teams in contemporary organizations energize themselves by means of the principle of self-giving. For that matter, no teamwork can happen without unconditional giving by team members. Team spirit is developed when giving happens spontaneously. Mother Teresa told her sisters in the Missionaries of Charity, "Give till it hurts." In organizational team work, members give their labor, their knowledge, and their attention. They also lend their ears and voices. Finally they give their hearts and their spirits. Leadership is the task of orchestration of the unique gifts that each team member brings to the organization. A leader's role is to turn the conditioned efforts of team members toward unconditional giving.

LEADERSHIP ROLE: FOSTERING UNITY IN DIVERSITY

I met Ms. Bobby Gutman, vice president for global diversity for Motorola, at a gathering of Fulbright scholars in Chicago. Gutman had moved around the world and had seen more diversity of cultures than most of us would ever see in a lifetime. She had something profound to say about the need for respecting diversity in the workplace. She said,

> Diversity is good business. Gray matter of the brain is not a monopoly of one culture or race or country. It is evenly distributed across the human population. So it makes sense to collect as much gray matter as possible in the interest of business.
>
> . . . Bobby Gutman

I had never heard of a more convincing reason for valuing diversity in organizations across the world. Gutman values the two principles of human relations in Motorola: (1) constant respect for people, (2) uncompromising integrity.

These are the two prerequisites for managing diversity in any organization anywhere. Respect for people is not cosmetic courtesy. It is not the proverbial, "When in Rome do as the Romans do." This respect means, *re-spect*. The syllable *spect* has the same root as *spectacle; spect* means to see. Re-spect therefore means to re-view, or to see again. Genuine respect only comes from the will to see a person not as a nodding acquaintance but as someone from whom we can learn, someone who is worthy of a second look. Respect is an attitudinal issue—it changes our attitude toward our co-workers and our neighbors. This kind of attitudinal change brings about greater harmony and promotes diversity.

Uncompromising integrity, which is a basic value for understanding diversity, comes from self-respect. Only when we learn to respect ourselves can we respect others. The self and the other are connected by a common value—the value of humanness. At a more profound level this common ground exists in our spiritual unity. The Dalai Lama, talking about his own realization about the interconnected reality of the self and the other said, "In fact, self and other are relative like this side of the mountain and that side of the mountain. From my perspective, I am self and you are other, but from your perspective, you are self and I am other" (Dalai Lama, 1995).

The Dalai Lama intuitively grasped a reality of organization that Peter Senge described in *The Fifth Discipline* as *systems thinking*. Senge is talking about "a framework for seeing interrelationship rather than things" (Senge, 1990). Such a framework cannot be found in the linear logic of thought, which invariably fragments reality into isolated things and understands diversity as division. We must be clear that diversity is different from division. Division comes from the analytic framework of thoughts. In division there is no connectedness between the divided parts. Every part is separate like chalk and cheese. In diversity, there exists between the diverse parts a subtle thread of unity. Man and woman represent not division but a diversity in Nature. Between man and woman there always is a possibility of unity.

This unity cannot be grasped with thought; it can be grasped with love alone.

To understand diversity, a leader must come out of the limiting circle of logic to the liberating circle of love. As a character in *The Little Prince* tells us: "It is only with the heart that one can see rightly; what is essential is invisible to the eye" (Saint-Exupery, 1971). Leaders in organizations have to shift their perspective from utility in diversity to a more radical feeling for unity in diversity.

Unity in diversity is the secret of Nature's organization. With this process, Nature keeps its various constituents in a state of dynamic equilibrium. In the organization of an ecosystem, the soil, the plants, the insects, and the animals exist as a rich diversity. Yet they are united in an interrelationship not only with each other but also with the system as a whole. The balance of unity in diversity is very dynamic. Each species in this ecosystem is evolving toward unity. This evolution is what we know as love.

In the patterns of organization created by human beings we see the replication of the quest for unity that all systems in Nature aspire toward. Senge wrote:

> In engineering, when an idea moves from an invention to an innovation, diverse "component technologies" come together. Emerging from isolated developments in separate fields of research, these components gradually form an "ensemble of technologies" that are critical to each other's success. Until this ensemble forms, the idea, though possible in the laboratory, does not achieve its potential in practice.
>
> ... Peter M. Senge, *The Fifth Discipline: The Art and Practice of Learning Organization*, 1990

Nurturing the environment of unity in which the component and complementary qualities of human beings can be brought together in a relationship constitutes the culture of diversity. The General Electric Company has espoused the cause of diversity by aspiring "To create a work environment that emphasizes our commitment to treating each other with dignity, trust and respect by recognizing each other's beliefs, values and differences" (Pollar and Gonzalez, 1994).

It is, however, not enough for leaders simply to recognize intellectually that a certain unity exists amid the diversity in their organizations. Leaders must feel this unity in their blood and in their bones. This feeling comes from *ekatmanubhuti*, the classical Indian expression that means unity of spirit. In this state of feeling leaders recognize that unity in diversity is the deep democracy that underlies Nature's organization. They then begin to value relationships within the organization as relationships of feeling as well as relationships of function. Leadership becomes an embodiment of *ekatmanubhuti*, unity of spirit, which is the ultimate human value.

Can the spiritual dimension of our relatedness be incorporated in the kind of organizations we encounter everyday? I have the example of one organization in which such a thing is happening. Here I wish to tell you the story of the biomedical company, Medtronic, Inc., in the words of its chief executive officer, Bill George:

> Medtronic was founded more than forty years ago by a spiritual leader named Earl Bakken. Sure Earl is a great inventor who created the first battery operated wearable pacemaker. He also is a great visionary who in 1960, when the company was near bankruptcy, wrote a mission statement that laid out Medtronic's future for the next hundred years. But even more important than that, Earl is still the spiritual leader, or "soul" of Medtronic, despite [the fact] that he has been retired for four years.
>
> The mission he wrote more than thirty years ago, not one word of which has been changed, calls for Medtronic to restore people to the fullness of life and health. Our 9,000 employees are totally dedicated to that mission, regardless of whether they work in the R & D lab, the factory, the accounting department, or in the hospital.
>
> Earl still meets with every new employee of Medtronic, all around the world. In these three hour sessions with 15 to 20 employees, he describes the founding and mission of the company, answers questions and then awards each employee a

medallion symbolic of his or her work with Medtronic. . . . Earl also carries his spirituality in the marketplace. You will find him at every major medical meeting around the world at the Medtronic exhibit from 8 A.M. until 6 P.M., talking to doctors young and old alike, about the importance of their work in saving lives with Medtronic products.

The latest focus in our organization is to stress "leading by values," rather than "management by objectives." We believe that if all of us, employees and managers alike, agree on the values that guide our work, employees can be fully empowered to realize them. This emphasis is especially important to the many self-directed work teams that are becoming the backbone of our organizational structure.

What are these values? They are, first of all, restoring people to full health; next serving our customers with products and services of unsurpassed quality; recognizing the personal worth of employees; making a fair profit and return for our shareholders; and maintaining good citizenship as a Company. Not surprisingly, these values are taken directly from the Medtronic system, which is well understood by all Medtronic employees. And the results of the past thirty years, or the past eight years, seem to validate that approach: $1,000 invested in 1960 in Medtronic stock would be worth $1.65 million today.

At Medtronic we don't mix religion and business, but we certainly do not shy away from the spiritual side of our work and the deeper meaning of our mission to save lives.

. . . Bill George, Medtronic, Inc.

HUMAN VALUES AND MANAGEMENT OF CHANGE

As most businesses around the world are becoming more and more global, the rhetoric of change is heard everywhere. Change and its management seem to have assumed unprecedented significance, especially in Asian businesses, which are tentatively stepping out into the glare of market economy from the shadowy worlds of government controls and a sheltered business environment.

In the backdrop of sharp discontinuities with the past modes of conducting business in some developing economies, one sees a crisis of vision and a rapid erosion of human values in the workplace. In the flurry of organizational changes that have come to mean commercialization of all human endeavors, there lurks the distinct possibility of loss of human identities in general and the submergence of cultural identities in particular. In the name of globalization, local human values and culture-bound insights are being swept off, resulting in psychological rootlessness and the loss of vital organizational energy.

After gaining independence from British rule in 1947, India sought to be transformed from a predominantly agrarian economy to a modern industrial nation. Jawaharlal Nehru, free India's first prime minister, had a vision of India as a nation with a pride of place in the world. Under Nehru's leadership India's gradual exposure to the West went hand in hand with large scale upgrading of technology. This brought into focus the emergent theme of management of change as an accompaniment of technological upheaval.

To begin with, such changes were brought about by means of designing new structures borrowed largely from contemporary and at times obsolete Western models. When patchwork models such as these failed to deliver, management systems based on coordination and control, once again imitative of the West, were introduced. Such structural and systems changes became increasingly dysfunctional as they ignored the basic dynamics and spirit of human values that are characteristic of the Indian soil.

For example, traditional organizations, which were run as Indian families with their indigenous psychological equations of relatedness to the organization, of respect for elders, and concern for younger members, sought to be infused with "modern" systems. The new systems were based on impersonal equations at work, dissolution of traditional hierarchies, and reliance on assumed contractual relationships—all of which were incongruent with the basic grain of the Indian psyche. The result has been a painful mismatch of roles and identities, of systems and people, of explicit strategies and implicit values.

Popular concepts in modern management such as quality circles, *kaizen*, and management by objectives and their assorted techniques are now being incorporated from abroad as potential solutions for meeting the challenges of change as India enters the global economy in the last decade of the present century. But the outcome has been management of crisis, management of chaos, or management of manipulating structures. Anything but management of change in the real sense of the term.

There have been exceptions to this pattern of managing change based on imitation of other successful models. Dr. V. G. Kurien, who pioneered India's cooperative farm movement, was instrumental in creating indigenous institutional structures for technical and socioeconomic change in the villages of Gujarat in western India. The most noteworthy of these institutions is known as the Anand Pattern of Cooperatives. Kurien's leadership philosophy is based on managing change through a synthesis of professional management and folk wisdom: "I believe our dairy and oilseed cooperatives have shown that when the energy and wisdom of our farmers are linked with professional management, there are no limits to what can be achieved" (Kurien, 1978).

The salient features of the Anand Pattern of Cooperatives are as follows:

1. They consist of a set of village cooperatives all of which commit themselves to the collective membership of a union of cooperatives.
2. The cooperatives select from among themselves a set of leaders whom they trust to protect the interests of the producer membership as a whole.
3. The cooperatives own facilities such as dairy plants. It is through these cooperatives that farmers can hire professionals like managers, technologists, and veterinary doctors.
4. The institutional structure serves as an instrument to bring modern technology in the service of the poorest of farmers.
5. Because these institutions are directed and controlled by the chosen representatives of the villagers who own them,

each farmer participates in the technical and socioeconomic changes.

6. These institutions have evolved their own value system that determines decision making. For example, a veterinary doctor who cannot cure animals or who does not arrive on time and an animal dies is dismissed. Similarly, a producer who conducts a private milk business "on the side" is ineligible to represent fellow members. There is therefore a reciprocal and automatic acceptance of disciplinary norms between the producer and the professional.

The overwhelming success of the Anand Pattern of Cooperatives in India and its growing international reputation have demonstrated a simple truth about effective management of change. The truth is that values-based institutions that evolve from the wisdom of the soil and recognize the right to self-determination of people can bring about enduring change.

Asian countries such as South Korea and Singapore have implemented change processes in their business organizations not by aping Western management practices but by a process of selective discrimination. They have been successful in unlocking the spontaneous reservoirs of energy of their people in their march toward modernity.

These traditional Eastern societies have remained cohesive by virtue of owning up to their collective ethos, which values group effort and group rewards. They have also responded to the dynamics of transformation not through quick, synthetic structural changes but through patience and perseverance in which individuals subordinate their selfish ambitions for the cause of the nation. In such societies systems of law are as important as intrinsic values-based leadership.

Francis Fukuyama's telling comment in his provocative book *The End of History and the Last Man* is worth mentioning here: "For us in the West, we have to wonder whether rather than being at a stage of evolution toward being more like us, Confucian Democracies have found a route towards 21st century modernity that we don't know about" (Fukuyama, 1992).

Whereas Confucian ethic is rightly extolled today as the source of east Asia's transformation from "undeveloped countries" to economically powerful nations, the less affluent countries such as India who have long chased the mirage of the West are beginning to do serious soul-searching about going back to their roots.

IDENTITY AND CHANGE: A HUMAN VALUES PERSPECTIVE

In Nature, all change processes take place on the foundation of continuity. The seasons change, spring follows winter, the day changes into dusk—all these follow the continuity of a time cycle. No change can be perceived without continuity. In organizations the system of bench-marking is an example of a standard of continuity against which progress is measured. The often-heard expression "Change is the only constant thing in today's world" ("Nothing endures but change." —Heraclitus) is itself a validation that change is preceded by a continuity of perspective that always endures.

In a human organization, change takes place on the enduring foundation of human identity. As human beings we accept change that enhances our sense of well-being—our identity. Any change that threatens our basic identity is resisted. That is the law of human nature. Keeping this hypothesis in mind, I would like to lay down the following ten postulates relating to management of change:

1. Any change process based predominantly on technoeconomic considerations to the oblivion of human values is likely to disrupt interpersonal and intrapersonal relationships within the organization.

2. Management of change must not only ensure that the basic harmony between human beings themselves is undisturbed but also that the equilibrium between human beings and Nature is maintained.

3. Resistance to change is not a necessary evil to be done away with. It has to be seen empathetically as the defense mechanism in human Nature to resist anything that threatens its identity.

4. Management of change not only should concern itself with changes in the behaviors, skill, and attitudes of people but also should seek to bring about more fundamental values-based transformation of people. This transformation includes both forward-looking innovation and retrospective restoration of good ideas of the past.

5. The basis for effecting change not only should be objective information and data collected as "facts" but also must include the subjective domain of wisdom, which springs from the culture of the soil.

6. Change necessitates a holistic, integrated approach to the problems of the organization conceived as an extension of larger communities such as society and country and cannot succeed only with isolated technical innovations.

7. Innovation of structure and technology must be preceded by alteration and enrichment of human consciousness. To change or not to change—that is a more decisive question than how to change.

8. Organizational values expressing beliefs, practices, and codes of conduct can be traced to underlying and often unconscious human values, which are culture-specific. They express a deeper reality and a purpose of existence for the organization and its members. Management of change must rediscover, sift, and re-create the deeper patterns of reality that exist beyond the structure of the organization and its immediate context.

9. An act of change creates a subtle tension between the existing order of things and the potential order that lies in the future. A leader who has to manage change must encounter this tension and consciously channel it toward greater harmony and consequently greater organizational effectiveness.

10. In this sense leaders who are change agents must operate from a state of consciousness that makes it possible to undergo self-transformation and self-renewal before they bring about real change in others. To go back to what Gandhi said, "I must first be the change I wish to see in my world" (Fischer, 1962).

Management of change must address itself to a rite of renewal whereby organizations can transcend the very rationale of their existence from a mundane to a spiritual plane—from mere discontinuity to greater continuity and harmony. This transcendence does not deny systems, procedures, or profits. But when all of them are acknowledged, enduring life-vision is affirmed by means of upholding deeper threads of continuity in the face of change. This continuity comes from core human values, myths, traditions of the past, and the soil and evolutionary history of a culture.

An organization, like a nation, also has an identity composed of the collective identities of its people and their beliefs, practices, and values. Systems can be acted on and structures can be manipulated, but an identity is almost impossible to erase. Management of change succeeds only when these identities are renewed time and again by means of building of institutions within the organization for individuals to use to replenish themselves and reclaim their essential spiritual heritage.

Leaders as agents of change need to explore the roots of this heritage from the supramundane history of the organization. Leaders have to ask, "What is that human spirit of enterprise that has brought the organization into being in the first place?" For those of us in leadership positions who are still skeptical about comprehending our past for the future of our present, I can do no better than quote these wonderful lines from a book called *The Scientific Outlook* by Bertrand Russell: "Men in the past were often parochial in space, but the dominant men of our age are parochial in time. They feel for the past a contempt that it does not deserve, and for the present a respect that it deserves still less" (Russell, 1931).

> This giving until it hurts—this sacrifice—is also what I call love in action. Every day I see this love—in children, men and women.
>
> ... MOTHER TERESA

7

Leadership and Love

LEADERSHIP: LOVE IN ACTION

My first meeting with Mother Teresa was at her home in Calcutta. I had gone there with a specific mission: to find out the secret of her success as the world's most well-known spiritual leader. The founder of the Missionaries of Charity, Mother Teresa had by then earned the formidable reputation of being "a living saint." I therefore approached her residence, located in a narrow lane in Calcutta, with a great deal of awe wondering how much of this celebrity leader I would get to know amid the rush of visitors who flocked to her everyday from all around the world.

I encountered a very unassuming woman in a white cotton Indian sari. The eighty odd years of age and pacemaker in her heart had not left their mark on her cheerful spirit. Her enthusiasm was child-like and infectious. Our eyes met. It was impossible not be impressed by the intensity of her look. We talked about the organization she was heading. She told me with quiet determination how she had established her mission in virtually all countries of the world and how difficult it was to set up an organization in China. She also told me in a good-humored manner how lucky she was to be able to travel free everywhere, because no airline would charge her airfare.

But what about the secret of your leadership, Mother? I was curious to know what made her, as described by the Secretary General of the United Nations, "the most powerful woman on earth." Her answer came to me as a revelation of an extraordinary kind: "Small work with great love." I thereafter often saw Mother Teresa as an embodiment of that very profound leadership philosophy—*small work with great love.*

I realized that physically it would be impossible to accomplish such great feats of human endeavor as building the Great Wall of China, conquering Mount Everest or, for that matter, building a successful multinational company unless there was sustained effort of an extraordinary kind. I wondered whether there was something intangible in the human constitution that made it possible to sustain such high-energy work? It became quite clear to me that the greatness of the effort comes from the intensity of love, which is the spirit behind the action. Leadership is the manifestation of the invisible energy of love expressed through the visible medium of action.

Bill George, chief executive officer of Medtronic, is an example of a corporate leader who subscribes to this leadership philosophy. Bill finds inspiration in the words of Kahlil Gibran, "Work is love made visible." It is possible to hear in Bill's voice the conviction of a person who has experienced the energy of love in his leadership work at Medtronic. In one of his presentations to business school students Bill goes on to quote the entire passage from Gibran as though he were saying an earnest prayer: "Work is love made visible. And if you cannot work with love but only with distaste, it is better that you should leave your work and sit at the gate of the temple and take alms of those who work with joy" (Gibran, 1970).

Bill completely identifies with the mission of Medtronic, which is "to help people lead fuller lives." He said, "We restore people to the fullness of life. That mission is easy for me to identify with." This intense identification with what one works for is what Mother Teresa calls small work with great love.

Love in the context of work is not a noun but is a verb. Love is not simply recognizing the objective value of a given work. It is rather the process of creating value in any work we do. Paying attention to details, giving greater energy to the process rather than to the outcome, and spontaneous involvement of the self in the work are the foundations of love in action. When we do small work with great love, our work automatically becomes great. Bill George experienced this as "the light shines in you—and you let others see it as well."

When we define love merely as a feeling, we do not recognize the infinite organizing capacity of love in our everyday lives. Love is the unifying principle that holds an atom together, creates magnetic and gravitational fields, and synchronizes the movement of planets in our physical universe. In our psychological universe, love generates our social and parental instincts, builds friendships, unites lovers, and creates affinity between people in organizations. In the larger spiritual realm, love raises the human organism beyond physical and social needs toward greater integration with the cosmos.

The creative balance of human civilization is maintained because of the equilibrium struck between self-interest and altruism, between our competition for survival and our cooperation for sustenance. One cannot even imagine a human society that relies merely on the logic of the survival of the fittest. Without the balancing factor of qualities such as cooperation and empathy even survival would be difficult. Our physical survival is linked to the cause and effect of giving and receiving. To the plant kingdom we give carbon dioxide and receive oxygen in return. Our psychological survival depends on care and consideration of others. Our spiritual survival depends on our sense of contact with a great reality that ensures our continuity beyond the temporal dimensions of life.

Love is the common value that is present in both our competitive and cooperative frames of reference. In competition, love becomes a means to achieve an end: as when we love our work because it will fetch us greater rewards than our colleagues. In cooperation, love becomes an end in itself, as when we love doing work for our families for no apparent reason other than the sheer experience of sharing ourselves with others.

Love is the evolutionary impulse that pushes us from a competitive mindset toward the instinct for cooperation. Beyond cooperation love evolves purely as a state of being that transcends the dichotomies of competition or cooperation. In this state we are in touch with the pure energy of love that holds the atom and the universe together. Love is uncontaminated energy that is not conditioned by outside reality. The Sufis express as follows their experience of pure love as an encounter with the divine:

> Love is His essence.
> Love is His presence.

Conscious leaders are aware of love in action. They know that if work is creation, love is the creative impulse behind it. These leaders trace the mysterious source of love not in the objective arena of action but within their own hearts. Love is not a mere feeling present on the surface of experience; it has to be traced to the depths of one's being and the ultimate source of one's great actions.

NATURE OF LOVE: THREE HABITS OF THE HEART

I am reminded again of the wonderful lines from *The Little Prince* that tell us about the nature of the heart:

> "Goodbye," said the fox. "And now here is my secret, a very simple secret: It is only with the heart that one can see rightly; what is essential is invisible to the eye."
> "What is essential is invisible to the eye," the little prince repeated, so that he would be sure to remember.
> ... ANTOINE DE SAINT-EXUPERY, *The Little Prince*, 1971

The heart has been acknowledged by masters of antiquity as a potential source of wisdom and intelligence. The sacred traditions held that a pure heart was the foundation for purity and clarity of perception. By the word *heart*, of course, the ancients did not mean the biologic heart. They were referring to the "heart center," which they understood as the seat of emotional intelligence. The great masters knew that emotions, like intellect, have to be cultivated. They therefore developed the three habits of the heart as important life skills. They are:

1. The habit of desire
2. The habit of passion
3. The habit of wholeness

First of all, we associate the heart with desire, as in the statement: "I ate to my heart's content." Desire is the first stirring of life in the biologic universe—it is the primary impulse for living. When the energy of desire works purely at the physical level, it is regulated by a control mechanism built into our physical nature. Our desire for water is quenched as soon the body's thirst is met. But the problem arises when desire overshoots the limit of the physical and trespasses into the mental world. This happens because the undigested physical experience leaves its residue on the mind in the form of memory. It is the memory of unfulfilled pleasurable sensation that gives birth to desire.

The mechanics of mental desire are as follows. When we experience a physical event through our five senses, we move in linear time. This movement arises with the beginning of the event and ends with the ending of the sensation of the event. When the experience of this sensation does not end with the event, the experience is transferred from the physical body to the mind, which still lives with the experience. This unfulfilled experience immediately becomes a part of memory. Whereas the physical event is an irreversible process in time, the experience as memory is reversible. This results in our desire for a pleasurable event long after the event is over. The lack of synchronicity between event and experience gives birth to this desire.

When our desire for a pleasant experience turns into a dysfunctional response of habit, we can conclude that our ardor has truly turned into addiction. Even our routine action can turn into addiction when we are unable to let go our mental engagement with work in which we are not physically engaged anymore. An example of this is mental tension from the workplace that we bring home with us. The action in the office has ceased, but the activity continues in our mind. This activity is energy dissipating. It continues as a subtle undercurrent of agitation in our memory and affects the quality of our work.

Conscious leaders act from the core of their hearts. Their desire for action is poured out in totality to the immediate context of action. They act here and now with great love. This way they master desire rather than become mastered by it. If this action is total and instantaneous, it does not spill over into activity and nervous agitation. It is then that the leader can claim to have cultivated the first habit of the heart—to channel the energy of desire along the path of the desirable.

The second way that the heart expresses itself is through passion. Passion is a sustained form of desire for something. When someone says, "I have a passion for music," she is expressing her long-term love for music. Passion is a quality of the heart. It is another form of love that consists of a sense of dissolution of self for something beautiful and inspiring. How does one cultivate passion? Can it be cultivated in the first place? Of this J. Krishnamurti says the following:

> Do not ask how to acquire passion. People are passionate enough in getting a good job, or hating some poor chap, of being jealous of someone, but I am talking of something entirely different—a passion that *loves*. Love is a state in which there is no *me*.
>
>   . . . KRISHNAMURTI, *On Learning and Knowledge*, 1994

In passion the heart of the leader rises from the flickering impulse of egocentric desire toward a steady flame of aspiration. When passion finds direction in a life-sustaining goal, leaders abandon the prompting of their egos and begin to live for the other. This is what Gandhi and Mother Teresa did when they discovered their passion for truth and service. Krishnamurti wrote the following:

> Love, I assure you, is passion. And without love, do what you will—follow this guru or that, read all the sacred books, become the greatest reformer, study Marx and have a revolution—it will be of no value, because when the heart is empty, without passion . . . there can be no self-abandonment.
>
> . . . KRISHNAMURTI, *On Learning and Knowledge,* 1994

The second habit of the heart is therefore to guide the flame of passion toward compassion. In leadership, compassion is the culmination of the leader's passion. In being compassionate leaders develop integral bonds of fellowship with their followers.

The third habit of the heart is that it sees everything in entirety and not in parts. The intellect of a human being computes form and phenomenon by means of the twin processes of fragmentation and analysis. Intellectual thoughts operate at a grosser level of the mind. This mind proceeds step by step as a mason who constructs a house brick by brick. Beyond the intellect, another subtle layer of mind is centered in the heart. This mind intuitively grasps a form as a master artist captures an entire landscape through illumined eyes. This is the secret of the habit of wholeness of the heart.

Wholeness is the result of an experience of unity within the Self. When we are united within ourselves we can see life in a multiplicity of dimensions. In wholeness, we do not see the mere surface of reality but probe the very depths. Wholeness is an experience; it is a feeling. Wholeness is returning to the center of our being. In the words of Lord Byron:

> I live not in myself, but I become
> Portion of that around me: and to me
> High mountains are a feeling . . .
> . . . LORD BYRON, *Childe Harold's*
> *Pilgrimage,* canto III, 1816

While seeing in fragments through our surface minds, we use only a small part of our capacity to see. It is like seeing a movie through still pictures. In wholeness we have a chance to experience the richness and dynamism of life. A corporate leader who is directly in touch with his subordinates and shakes hands with them once in a while is experiencing wholeness. If the same leader were to be acquainted with his subordinates through their biographic data in computer printouts, he would experience only a fragment and not a whole person. Albert Einstein was describing the rare experience of wholeness when he said that small is the number of them that see with their own eyes and feel with their own hearts.

The three habits of the heart enable conscious leaders to chose the path of the desirable from those of many desires; they energize these leaders to transform passion into all-embracing compassion, and they empower these leaders to see life as an interdependent wholeness rather than as a heap of broken images.

FROM HIGH-TECH TO HIGH-TOUCH LEADERSHIP

> The master said to the businessman: "As the fishes perish on dry land, so you perish when you get entangled in the world. The fish must return to the water—you must return to solitude."
>
> The businessman was aghast. "Must I give up my business and go into a monastery?"
>
> "No, no. Hold on to your business and go into your heart."
>
> . . . KENNETH GOODPASTER

This beautiful anecdote comes from a former Harvard professor, a man with a truly big heart, Kenneth Goodpaster. I learned lessons in ethical leadership from Ken and realized that leadership is not cerebral but is a hands-on experience. Ken has the busiest of schedules, traveling from one part of the world to another, teaching, running corporate seminars, and finding time for his family. Yet in my year-long association with him, I always saw him attending to the smallest of things as though each task were was all that mattered to him. At the end of a meeting he would clear empty coffee cups from the table when everyone had left. Looking at the way Ken negotiates his life and work, I realized that a conscious leader may think in abstract ideas, but he lives with his attention focused on concrete details.

The secret of high-touch leadership is simply this: paying attention to and lending your heart to details. In contemporary leadership, there is a declining market for lofty speeches and noble thoughts. All followers want to see is a life lived in detail, according to stated principles. Followers' perceptions of leaders are not made up of the halos around them but of infinitesimal details of day-to-day living.

A touch is a powerful medium of communication in our lives. Leaders who are conversant with the language of touch know that it produces a deep impact on the mind of the person who receives the touch. Touch can be purely physical, as in shaking hands, but the emotional impact of even a physical touch is unmistakable. Leaders' hands can be powerful messengers of their emotions. Followers respond in the physical and emotional sense by saying: "Oh! I was touched by her kind gesture."

Earl Bakken of Medtronic understands the importance of high-touch leadership as he travels the world from Minneapolis to Tokyo meeting each of his nine thousand employees in small groups of fifteen to twenty people at a time. The employees value their leader's gift of touch. Relationships endure in Medtronic as a result of this. Every Fourth of July, Linda Marcelli, district director at Merrill Lynch, treats hundreds of her support staff with food she cooks herself. For her it is a "labor of love." Linda is someone who believes in the power of high-touch leadership. She says, "If one of my financial consultants is having a problem, I'll put my arm around him."

In the evolution of human consciousness, touch plays a significant role. Most of our information in infancy and childhood comes through the medium of touch. As we age and begin to lose our senses, it is the sense of touch that persists even when all the other senses have become dull. We literally and figuratively grasp the essence of reality through touch.

The dimensions of the sense of touch go beyond the physical and psychological planes. Most ancient civilizations were aware of the spiritual aspect of touch. In India, the essential spiritual nature of touch was known as *sparsa tattva*. Spiritual wisdom from the master to the disciple was sometimes communicated through *sparsa*, or touch. The tradition of healing in many ancient cultures involved a conscious use of touch. Although touch is a forgotten art today, modern medical research does recognize the therapeutic value of touch. Recent research has shown that babies who are touched more often by their parents develop better physical and psychological health when they grow up.

Leaders who believe in the value of high touch also see the impact of touch on their colleagues. These leaders transmit their energy and enthusiasm to whomever they touch. And this transfer of energy does not necessarily have to be through a physical touch. It can happen through a caring glance, or even a gentle look of approval. It can happen through a handwritten anniversary wish or even a silent moment of sharing with a colleague who has undergone a personal tragedy.

Gandhi understood the importance of high-touch leadership in a human organization. He said, "Work with the hands is the apprenticeship of honesty. May the work of your hands be a sign of gratitude and reverence to the human condition." Great leaders like Gandhi think of their hands not only as an instrument of the body and mind but also as spiritual partners. Whether it is a handshake or an Indian *namaste*, the introductory face-to-face meeting between two human beings often involves the use of hands. Both are profound gestures that build bridges of understanding between people.

Leaders in our highly technological society have tended to keep touch with reality through impersonal push-button systems. Relationships built through high-tech methods such as faxes and e-mail have their own advantages, because they standardize and economize on the cost and time of communication. But in this quest for standardization of communication procedures, leaders miss out on the uniqueness of old-fashioned human touch. William Hauser, head of the technical department at AT&T for several years, told me how he felt the loss of human contact with the advent of e-mail communication. An old-timer with AT&T, Hauser has experienced how people come together less and less in their offices and prefer e-mail or teleconferencing from their homes. This, he understands, has resulted in the loss of value of human touch in the organization.

Leaders like Hauser are not alone in their perception of the problem arising out of high-tech communication systems. It is interesting that with the introduction of cellular phones and pagers, which increase mobility in communication, there seems to be a greater urge for staying in touch among the high-tech leaders of today. Network communication has created a paradoxic situation by making human contact impersonal while at the same time bringing more and more people together in the network. This, I feel, is an indication that even the instruments of technology have responded to an utterly human need: the need for intimacy.

LEADERSHIP AND INTIMACY:
THE FEMININE CONSCIOUSNESS

An organization is a web of intimate relations. The organization is greater than the sum of its constituent parts not because the parts are merely added on but because they are related. The organization as a whole is a relational pattern that remains even when individual members come and go. The leaves of a tree grow and die every season, but the dynamic pattern of the whole tree remains. The intimate relation that exists between individuals within an organization has therefore as much substance as the individuals themselves. This undefinable energy of intimacy is a factor that determines the effectiveness of leadership.

Intimacy is a state of awareness. It is not simply physical proximity. Two people can be intimate even when they are thinking on the same wavelength. It requires a special quality of consciousness to be truly intimate. I would like to describe this special quality as *receptivity*. There are a rich repertoire of attributes of the quality of receptivity. The ability to listen, the virtue of patience, the art of accommodating and understanding a person in context, and the willingness to allow emotion and intuition to guide decision making—these are some of the factors of receptivity. The quality of receptivity is a refined form of instinct among human beings that helps in accurate processing of information. It allows an individual to be more intimate with contextual details of information.

"I follow my instincts. You don't always see your path until you get there," said Rebecca Mark, chief executive officer of the global energy company Enron Development Corporation. When the local government in India canceled Enron's two billion dollar power project in India, Rebecca became instrumental in resurrecting the deal. This was done in the face of the stiff governmental opposition and adverse public opinion that the project had generated. It was a remarkable turnaround for a business that few chief executive officers would even think of reviving. Mark was able to bring about through persuasion what Enron's financial clout could not do. It was a triumph of a receptive instinct over raw organizational power.

Receptivity nurtures the spirit of accommodation. Rebecca Mark said, "I am constantly asking, How far can I go? How much can I do?" Receptivity is the ability to push the limits of our capacity to absorb and accept reality. Receptivity is the polar opposite of the motives of power and aggression. Receptivity comes not from the love of power but from the power of love. It empowers one in spirit. None other than Napoleon Bonaparte acknowledged the power of the spirit over force in the last days of his life. He said: "Do you know what astonished me the most in the world? The inability of force to create anything. In the long run, the sword is always defeated by the spirit."

The feminine consciousness is truly receptive. It accepts, tolerates, and transforms. The feminine embraces the aggressive impulse of the outgoing masculine energy and transforms it into a higher order of creativity. The wind has a soft and invisible presence, yet it can move mountains of sand when blowing through a desert. Water is gentle and can be easily contained, yet it can carve out its pathway through stones. Lao-tzu used the wonderful analogy of water to convey the power of the feminine consciousness:

In the whole world there is nothing softer and weaker than water. And yet nothing measures up to it in the way it works upon that which is hard. Nothing can change it. Everyone on earth knows that the weak conquers the strong and the soft conquers the hard.

. . . *Tao Te Ching*

I must make it clear that feminine consciousness is an attribute that is not exclusive to the female sex. It is a state of consciousness that exists as a law of Nature and cuts across sex lines. Jesus Christ on the cross is the highest embodiment of the feminine power of tolerance over brute force. Gandhi epitomized the soft but unyielding force of nonviolence over aggression. A state of tolerance and nonviolence contains greater energy than a violent action, just as it requires greater capacity to stop a speeding car than to start it.

Leadership requires the capacity to absorb the conflicting energies of group members. This shock-absorbing mechanism makes it possible for the leader to be a confluence of diverse energies. By embodying the receptive quality of feminine consciousness, leaders consolidate the dissipative energy of their organization for greater effectiveness.

All organizations develop themselves through two broad phases. The first is the phase of conquest, and the second is the phase of consolidation. Conquest represents expansion of energy by means of building more capacity, capturing new markets, increasing human power, innovating technology, creating new products, and raising more capital. Consolidation represents conservation of energy through developing core competencies, retraining the existing workers, improving the quality of existing products, and increasing capacity utilization.

Organizations, like military maneuvers, progress in the rhythm of conquest and consolidation. Conquest is the rhythm of the masculine consciousness. Consolidation follows the law of the feminine consciousness. Leaders are in touch with this rhythm. By embodying both the masculine and the feminine aspects of consciousness, leaders intuitively know when to conquer and when to consolidate.

In their book *Brainsex*, Anne Moir and David Jessel describe what they call "the maternalistic style of management." They say that while men go by what is the right thing to do, women more often than not ask: what is the responsible thing to do? Whereas men are involved in relationship of functions, women are involved in relationship of feeling: "It is difficult for the male mind to comprehend the greater input of data—factual as well as emotional—which makes the female decision making a more elaborate, lengthy and balanced affair" (Moir and Jessel, 1989).

Some cultures have in the course of their evolutionary history created the identity of the feminine in terms of greater resilience and receptivity. In a culture like that of India, highly qualified women assuming leadership positions in all spheres of society acknowledge this social-historical factor in determining their leadership quality. Says Anu Aga, Chief Executive of the large Indian manufacturing company, Thermax: "In our society, women have to adapt quite a lot, to that extent, resilience comes in. For example, in most Indian families, a woman lives in her husband's home. As a result she has to adjust tremendously."

In traditional societies like that of India, in which a woman's household work has no cash value, there is increasing pressure on women to work in offices and then come home to work what may be called in factory parlance a second shift. This has brought about a remarkable shift in Indian women's perspective on leadership. These women lead not only by being resourceful at home but also by assuming new responsibilities in the office. Responsibility is a newly discovered leadership trait among Indian women. It was not as if women were not responsible at home, but this responsibility was hitherto unrecognized as something that has real value.

I will venture to tell you now the story of a young working woman who lives in Bombay, western India. Through her voice we shall hear how by being receptive to the pressures of working two shifts, home and office, she has found for herself a greater freedom to act. This sense of freedom of action has come with a price; she has to cope and adapt more. Her quest for corporate leadership is a remarkable demonstration of resilience that is characteristic of feminine consciousness. Here is an intimate glance at a day in the life of an Indian working woman:

This is a story of a ten-to-five woman. Let us call her Sangeeta. She works in an advertising agency. She is thirty, maybe thirty-five. It is difficult to tell her age by looking at her. Her youth, like the sunset, lingers rather coyly on her face. And her features, untouched by powder and the combined assault of lipstick and mascara, have a certain freshness of appeal.

Sangeeta is one among a quaint, quiet workforce that rushes through the city's commercial jungle from ten to five everyday. Day after day—a procession of pigtails, ponytails, vermillioned heads, and vanity bags. There is a certain rhythm in Sangeeta's walk that sets her apart from the drab work-a-day city people. If you watch her closely enough you can see the spectacle-scarred bridge of her nose and a pair of bright, trusting eyes. Eyes that glow like traffic lights, and you seem to know exactly when to go ahead with the introduction.

I strike up a conversation with her. "What makes a working woman work?" I ask her, thinking I have posed a very intelligent question. But Sangeeta's answer is as sharp as her aquiline nose, "That what makes a barking housewife bark—the desire for self expression." Amused by her reply, I decide to accompany her to her office.

I find her desk cluttered with colored pencils, half-finished sketches, scraps of paper, and odds and ends. On the wall is a prominent advertisement for a mosquito repellent which reads: Freedom at Midnight. "In the advertising profession we make you chase the impossible," she says with a half-suppressed giggle. It seems rather ironic to me that the working woman does precisely that all her life—chase the impossible.

Sangeeta has to run a domestic marathon in the house. This is followed by a sprint to her place of work. And finally, those endless hurdles in the office. I have found out that peeling a pineapple is a far more difficult undertaking than preparing a balance sheet. Having fared miserably in both these jobs, I feel my heart beating for the woman who does it all with such grace.

I marvel at the way a working woman combines cold professionalism with the warmth of home. She contributes to the fine art of management with her natural abilities and can straighten a ruffled workplace with a simple design—a manufactured smile.

Sangeeta is meanwhile absorbed in her job. Her nimble fingers work tirelessly to produce advertising copy. For a moment she raises her eyelashes as she tells me about her home. "At home there is my husband who is a jolly good fellow when everything is going right for him. But every time there is a little problem, the fellow behaves like a buffalo in a beauty parlor. I think every man wants to be a Napoleon before his wife. And every fight has to fought in the battlefield called home." Seeing her nostrils flare up in anger, I discreetly switch the subject.

"How many children have you?" I ask. "Oh! I am the mother of a three-year-old monster and there is another one in the pipeline. I don't know what he will turn out to be. My son is a riot! He has inherited his father's habit of shaking up the whole world for a small matter. Everybody takes a mother's patience for granted. No one considers that she is also a human being and has a right to revolt at times. People think that a working woman is dancing a ballet in the office. They are never willing to take us seriously. Neither at home nor in the world outside." Sangeeta pauses for a deep breath.

I can feel her frustration. And her agony of always having to put on appearances in a sad, madman's world. She walks the tightrope of life where a little lapse means falling from grace. She may smile demurely but not run like a man. She may gossip but not long enough to be suspected of having an affair. The working woman must struggle to play the mother, the worker, the nurse, and the soothing paramour. And she must struggle to remain forever beautiful. Her glory thrives on the mystique of her youth and beauty. She lives in the fear that her magic may not survive the ravages of time and tide. The very thought that she may have to live the life of a recluse far away from the spotlights haunts her.

As I ponder over all these, the telephone rings on Sangeeta's table. She picks up the receiver and listens anxiously. She acknowledges the caller's instructions with an occasional, "Yes, Sir" to fill up the conversation. Putting back the receiver in a short while she says, "My director. He has just asked me to go and meet a client. My little fellow is not well. I thought of going home early today. But my work is very important. I must go now."

While she prepares to go, this working woman appears to me as a walking enigma. I am amazed at the dexterity with which she switches roles. Before we part, Sangeeta smiles at me wistfully, "When you write about me tell your readers that I am more than just a pretty face. Tell them, I am a freedom fighter." I can only mutter an awed "Yes, Sir!"

LEADERSHIP: THE WAY OF UNCONDITIONAL LOVE

Someone once asked Abraham Lincoln, "Why do you love your enemies when you should destroy them?" To this Lincoln said: "Madam, do I not destroy them when I make them my friends."

Lincoln's way was the way of unconditional love. Love simply is. It is neither conditioned with the mind nor constructed with thought. It has no polar opposite. Hatred is not the opposite of love, for love knows no opposition. Love is a state of self-existent wholeness. It is pure energy that sustains relationships between form and phenomenon of existence. Hatred has no existential reality. It is merely make-believe mental conditioning. Hatred has no real presence, it is merely the absence of love. When love is, hatred is not.

Can a leader cultivate unconditional love? Perhaps not. Anything that is cultivated becomes a conditioned response of the mind. It does not remain unconditional. So how does one experience unconditional love then? This can be done simply by means of witnessing and overcoming our conditioning. We simply have to remove the mental blocks that impede the free-flowing stream of love. Saying "this man is a devil incarnate" and "that woman is totally heartless" are examples of the conditioning in day-to-day life that prevents us from loving. Or we may become stuck in frozen frames of our preconceived notions about people and cultural stereotypes and of our personal preferences. All these are barriers to experiencing unconditional love.

In organizations we often see interest groups, coteries, and cliques. All these groups only help distort the flow of unconditional love within organizations. They display self-serving behavior patterns, uphold prejudicial views of people, and undermine authentic relationships among the members of the organization. Leaders who succumb to such vicious circles of self-interest lose touch with unconditional love. When they transcend artificial divisions created by cravings of power and prejudice, these leaders find themselves in love again. J. Krishnamurti wrote:

> When we remove the division between the "me" and the "you,"
> the "we" and the "they," what happens? Only then and not
> before can one perhaps use the word "love." And love is that
> most extraordinary thing that takes place when there is no "me"
> with its circle or wall.
>
> . . . J. KRISHNAMURTI, *On Learning and Knowledge*, 1994

The wall that separates individuals within an organization is nothing but the circumference of a circle the center of which is the ego. If this center did not exist, there would be no circumference, no boundary to separate one individual from another. Conscious leaders understand the process of dissolving their ego boundaries as a way of realizing unconditional love. Said Bill George of Medtronic:

> One of the things you have to do in this whole process is to find a way to get egos out of the way, and it has to start with the CEO. People at the top of very large organizations have strong egos. That's not just true of business. It exists in Congress, medicine, law.
> . . . BILL GEORGE, Medtronic, Inc.

In organizations, a leader wields power in three distinct ways. The first is the *way of fear*. It is the basis of all kinds of dictatorship. Hitler assumed power through intimidation. His power was coercive and based on the fear-psychosis that he was able to transmit among the masses. Fear allows a leader to maintain temporary control but never a lasting relationship. The shadow side of fear is hatred. They go together. Leaders who lead through generating fear also earn hatred—this is natural law.

The second way of leadership is the *way of the carrot and the stick*. This is leadership by means of reward and punishment. In industrial organizations, money, perks, and promotions determine the carrot part and the stick comes from denials, dismissals, and cold-shouldering. This is a fairly safe way of getting the work done but it does not ensure that the best possible work is done. By adopting the carrot and stick approach, leaders induce in their followers the shortest route to success—seeking pleasure and avoiding pain. The obvious danger of following this route is that human beings are reduced to stimulus-response mechanisms. They work merely for utility and not out of genuine inspiration.

The third way of leadership is the way of *unconditional love*. A leader does not abandon discipline and punishment in loving unconditionally. But the very motive for the leader's disciplining the follower is genuine love. The leader is like the archetypal mother who disciplines the child only for the sake of the child's welfare. She is not the mother who demands return on investment for herself; she doesn't even demand gratitude from the child. She merely loves without imposing any condition. When leaders can love their followers this way, they do not have to seek out performance from their teams. Performance comes naturally from followers who give their best out of a sense of belonging and trust. Their work then truly becomes a labor of love.

The metaphor of the gardener comes in handy for understanding the path of unconditional love. The gardener understands the secret of producing a good crop of flowers. He looks at his garden as an extension of his self. He waters the plants regularly. He uses his pruning knife to remove weeds to facilitate growth. He denies excess sunshine to fledgling plants and protects them from the sun. He tills the soil, adds manure, and nurtures the garden with his whole heart. He doesn't force the flowers to bloom; they simply bloom by themselves in their own time. They unfurl their colors, spread their fragrance, their unique talents in response to the gardener's unconditional love.

Conscious leaders are like the gardener who simply facilitates growth. All they do is love unconditionally as the rain that falls in equal measure on hills and valleys. These leaders do not stop to ponder whether someone deserves their love. Loving without expectation of return brings its own rewards. Leaders have a sense of gratitude and fulfillment that there is someone to receive their love. Their joy is no less than that of the gardener who after a season of hard work sees his own energy manifest in a riot of colors. Each flower stands as a living testimony of love's labor.

The book of Nature is like a page written over or printed upon
with different-sized characters and in many different languages,
interlined and cross lined, and with a great variety of marginal
notes and references. There is coarse print and fine print. . . . It is a
book which he reads best who goes most slowly or even tarries
long by the way.

. . . JOHN BURROUGHS

8

Nature's Manuscript:
The Leadership Manual

CONSCIOUSNESS IN NATURE

It was a practice among rulers in ancient India to retreat into forests to renew their perspective on worldly matters. In the quietude of the forest, they could ponder, reflect and launch
themselves on a journey of self-discovery. This retreat was an
important phase in the entire life of a person of the world and
was known in ancient times as *vanaprastha*, or the "phase of the
forest." It was believed by ancient masters that there was consciousness in the hidden depths of Nature. And this consciousness was accessible to a human being who could enter into
intimate communion with the language of Nature.

There is a wonderful Chinese parable called "The Sound of
the Forest" translated by W. Chan Kim and Renee Mauborgne. It
describes the lessons learned by a young prince called T'ai in China
in the third century A.D. The essence of the parable is as follows:

*King Ts'ao sent his son Prince T'ai to the great master Pan Ku to learn
the basics of good leadership. When the Prince arrived before the master,*

169

he was advised by the master to go alone to the Ming-Li Forest. After one year the Prince was asked to return to the master and describe to him the sound of the forest.

After spending months in the forest, when Prince Ta'i returned, Pan Ku asked him to describe all that he could hear. Replied the Prince, "I could hear the cuckoos sing, the leaves rustle, the hummingbirds hum, the crickets chirp, the grass blow, the bees buzz, and the wind whisper and holler." Even before the Prince could finish, the master told him to go back to the forest and find out what more he could hear.

Puzzled by the master's whims, Prince Ta'i returned to the forest again. For days he heard no sounds other than what he had heard before. Then, one morning as he sat silently beneath the trees, he started to be conscious of faint sounds he had never heard before. The more keenly he listened, the clearer the sounds became. Slowly a new light of wisdom dawned on him and he decided to return to Pan Ku.

The master asked him what more he had heard. The Prince responded with reverence, "I could hear the unheard—the sound of flowers opening, the sound of the sun warming the earth, and the sound of the grass drinking the morning dew." Pan Ku was delighted that his disciple had found the secret of the forest and said: "To hear the unheard is necessary to be a good leader."

. . . CHINESE PARABLE,
translated by W. Chan Kim and Renee Mauborgne

In the unheard language of Nature there is absolute unity of sound and meaning. There is a purity of expression in the sound of the forest that cannot be found in the misleading voices of concrete corporate jungles. All of Nature is in fact an effusion of unheard language. Only human beings limit this flow through social conditioning. If we have keen ears we can hear the timeless vibrations of truth in the rustle of the leaves, in the buzzing of the bees or in the rippling waters of a river. Nature articulates the vibratory structure of all forms of this earth within the unitary stream of consciousness.

The Sanskrit word *mantra* best describes the language of conscious Nature. A *mantra* is not a mystic formula. It is the original form of language in which sound and meaning completely correspond. The language of *mantra* can be coherently understood in terms of its prime root meanings. These roots do not have meanings with rigid boundaries—they generally are intelligent vibrations of sound that help create meanings and give form to the formless.

Dr. David Frawley, an eminent scholar of Vedic sciences, tells us in his book, *Wisdom of the Ancient Seers*, that *mantras*

> . . . reflect a way of being that manifests on all levels, a quality of energy, a spectrum or vibratory range of meaning that has a certain characteristic but no single indication. They are like prime numbers from which complex equations can be evolved, but into which they are always resolvable.
>
> . . . DAVID FRAWLEY, *Wisdom of the Ancient Seers*, 1992

The Sanskrit root *stha* and the English root sound *st* evolve from the same original sound, which indicates stability. They have given rise to such allied English words as *stay, still, stop, stand, stable,* and *stall* and similar Sanskrit words such as *stithi* and *sthan*.

All of Nature is replete with *mantra*, which is nothing but primal sound undistorted by the mechanical noises of our civilization. Vibration of sound is a vivid expression of consciousness in Nature. Sound is also the maker of material reality of the world. When we are intimate with primal sounds or *mantra* we become co-creators of material reality. Leaders who hear the unheard voice of Nature enter into a different plane of consciousness. In this consciousness they are able to penetrate deep into the unspoken voices of people and develop insights into human nature.

Often we assume that we possess consciousness. The truth, however, is that consciousness possesses us. All we need to do is to allow the consciousness in our nature to function through us. Human consciousness is only a microcosm of Nature's supreme consciousness. The human body, which is a marvelous instrument, has evolved through thousands of years of tireless effort by conscious Nature. The human mind, which has conceived and given birth to awe-inspiring civilizations, has itself been shaped in the embryo of cosmic consciousness. Rabindranath Tagore expressed this in delightful language:

> The same stream of life that runs through my veins night and day runs through the world and dances in rhythmic measures.
>
> It is the same life that shoots in joy through the dust of the earth in numberless blades of grass and breaks into tumultuous waves of leaves and flowers.
>
> It is the same life that is rocked in the ocean-cradle of birth and of death, in ebb and in flow.
>
> I feel my limbs are made glorious by the touch of this world of life. And my pride is from the ebb-throb of ages dancing in my blood this moment.
>
> . . . RABINDRANATH TAGORE

In our human-centered world of corporations we have progressively marginalized Nature as an inert resource. The predatory prowl of technology has made our lives comfortable, but at the same time it has removed us from our own natures. The mystery and sanctity of the human-Nature relationship has been torn asunder by the all-knowing rational mind, which knows precious little about its own origin.

Leadership on the threshold of the twenty-first century needs to pause and ponder Nature's manuscript. Even in the mad rush for technological progress, leaders have to reflect on the timeless wisdom of Nature's ways. A leader need not be a romantic visionary to appreciate the marvelous precision and harmony in Nature's management. It is a harmony born out of a sheer quest for truth and beauty—a search for symbiosis and an unerring instinct for unity in diversity.

A conscious leader realizes that Nature never stands up like an egotistic demon and says, "I am the monarch of all I survey." Even the tallest tree recognizes with humility its debt to the soil. Elements of Nature hardly ever exploit one another as passive resources. They do not dominate or plunder each other in self-seeking madness. All of Nature is conscious of the fact that in the welfare of all is the welfare of one. Therefore Nature is consciously seeking to replenish and share whatever it has taken away. The cloud gives back to the earth in the form of rain what it has taken from the sea. The flower knows that the bee is not a burden but is a co-worker in its life's journey.

THREE LAWS OF LEADING CONSCIOUSLY

Nature is an endless combination and repetition of a very few laws. She hums the old well-known air through innumerable variations.

... RALPH WALDO EMERSON

When we come out of the complex maze of corporate life to look at the vast expanse of Nature, we are struck by the stark simplicity of the natural world. This simplicity is neither monotonous nor monochromatic. There is a tremendous diversity of color and sound in Nature's organization. Yet there is a discernible effortlessness with which Nature maneuvers this diversity of form and phenomena into a harmonious whole. Like a capable leader, Nature produces the most stunning of results with very modest means.

A spider's web is an example of marvelous organization in Nature. The web starts with a simple Y-shaped structure made from the secretion of the spider. The spider spins around this basic structure to produce a web of increasing subtlety. There is tremendous flexibility and adaptability in the spider's organization. When the web is partly or fully destroyed by an external agent, such as a breeze, the spider is quickly able to repair the damage and rebuild the web. If the breeze is of high intensity, the spider is able to build a web with thicker layers of silk that can withstand the onslaught. The spider on its web displays a discipline and order that the leader as the architect of an organization will find worthy of emulation.

Leadership in Nature's organization emerges from a consciousness that can comprehend the whole. To be able to comprehend the whole, this consciousness has to be aware of the relations between things and their contexts and not merely between things themselves. One fundamental difference between a human-made organization and Nature's organization is this: a person usually changes the context to suit things, whereas Nature changes things to suit a context. To cite an example, in the context of a cold climate, Nature creates plant and animal life that can withstand cold. When human beings build houses in cold climates they try to alter the conditions of the cold by making provisions for insulation and central heating systems. Whereas Nature places more emphasis on the entire context, human beings tend to subordinate the whole for the survival of the parts.

The greatest challenge that faces leadership today is to be able to strike a balance between the sustenance of the entire context of an organization while nurturing individual identities. The environmental and ethical concerns of modern organizations point toward the same dilemma. I believe only Nature has an answer to this riddle of relation between part and whole. For this we need to look at three laws of conscious leadership, which I have drawn from Nature's manuscript. These laws are as follows:

1. The law of complete concentration
2. The law of detached awareness
3. The law of transcendence

The first of these laws is the *law of complete concentration*. Concentration enables Nature to achieve a purity of purpose. This purity comes from arrangement of disorganized elements of Nature into one coherent whole. A solution of salt water left to itself exhibits this natural phenomenon. In the solution the dissolved components of the salt tend to concentrate into salt crystals, which is nothing but pure salt.

Purity is strength, and concentration is the mechanics of building this strength. The small acorn concentrates within it all the energy and information needed to grow a giant oak tree. A star athlete concentrates his entire energy on a specific group of muscles, which gives him power to overcome his opposition. A corporate leader concentrates on core competencies within her organization, which provide great leverage for the success of her organization.

What separates a human being from an animal is the degree of concentration. A dog cannot learn music or English, simply because the dog cannot concentrate on a subject for a sustained length of time. Similarly, the difference between an ordinary human being and an Albert Einstein is the degree of concentration that an Einstein brings to his work. When leaders concentrate on a thing or an idea for a sustained length of time, they generate a great amount pure energy. Through the power of natural law, leaders are able to harness this energy in the service of the organization.

Concentration in the context of mental functioning can be defined as the natural ability of the mind to remain focused on an object or thought. How does one cultivate complete concentration? Most spiritual traditions of the world have developed practices for cultivating total concentration of the mind. The Yoga tradition of Hinduism has defined one-pointedness of mind as the state of *ekagra*. One Yogic practice is to bring back order in the chaotic traffic of thoughts by concentrating the mind on the breath.

I dwell on this exercise at length in the next few pages. In the Theravada Buddhist tradition, the discipline of cultivating one-pointed attention is known as *samatha*. In the Islamic tradition, the word *dhikr* is used to denote developing the power of concentration by repeating the names of Allah. In the Jewish tradition, the expression *kavanah* means a concentrated form of prayer that induces an altered state of consciousness.

It is easy to concentrate our mind on something that appeals to our senses, such as a beautiful face or a flavorful food. But to achieve the same quality of concentration on the mundane things of life requires a certain discipline of the mind. It is the same discipline that helps us to train our memory in childhood.

Being attentive to the smallest of our actions, such as walking or breathing, makes it possible for our habitually scattered mind to gather together regularly. With constant practice it becomes easy for the mind to be drawn inward into one-pointed attention. Just as an archer pulls his arrow toward himself to shoot accurately and powerfully, a mind that is pulled to an inward focus becomes an effective instrument for outward action.

Conscious leaders know that concentration is the shortest road to achieving anything. To concentrate is to find one's own self. The art of concentration is in acquiring the capacity to withdraw one's consciousness from all things except the one, single goal toward which one is striving. Once leaders have learned the "how" of concentration, they can concentrate on anything effortlessly.

The second law of conscious leadership is the *law of detached awareness*. This seems like a paradoxic state: how can one be aware of something yet remain detached? Whenever I am asked to explain this point in my leadership workshops, I use an analogy taught to me by my teacher. "Imagine," I say, "the hand of a mother holding on to the hand of a two-year old who has just learned to walk. The mother has to soften her grip enough to enable the child to walk freely. But she has to be firm enough to ensure that the child does not lose balance."

When we concentrate too hard on some thing or some thought, we tend to put up an energy wall of resistance against total awareness. For example, when we struggle to listen to an announcement in a busy subway train, we try hard to tune out other noises. In this effort we lose some energy in building a resistance to what we consider undesirable noise. But those who have learned the discipline of concentrating their thoughts on a thing or an idea for a considerable period of time do not feel the need to resist anything from invading their awareness. We know of leaders who can stay focused even in the middle of noise and disturbance. They can concentrate on something specific and yet be aware of their entire surroundings.

J. Krishnamurti described this state of consciousness as "choiceless awareness." According to Krishnamurti, choiceless awareness is a fundamental psychological transformation that can be developed through nonjudgmental and nonreactive attention to everyday events. In the flame of pure attention, both outer events and inner experiences are brought under clear focus. The observer becomes detached from the act of observation. In this detachment attention is total.

The law of detached awareness enables leaders to enter a deeper state of attention. In this attention leaders reach beyond the dimensions of thought to a state of unconditioned consciousness. Here thinkers no longer try to focus on a certain thought. They simply are detached witnesses to the traffic of thoughts, mere bystanders. The thinker is a witness not a judge. No longer affected by her thoughts, the thinker can see them come and go like clouds in a sky.

At this stage thoughts begin to diminish in number; the gaps between successive thoughts become bigger. These gaps are like the waveless ocean of infinite silence. This silence has no name and no form. The domain of the nameless and formless is what unconditional awareness is all about.

All of Nature experiences unconditional awareness. The bird knows no name for the sky, it simply is aware of a vast expanse where it is free to move. The bee does not recognize the complex form of a flower; it simply is aware of where the honey is. In naming we create a wall between reality and our experience of it. When we name a tree as a tree, we separate it from the soil, which is an inseparable part of the ecosystem of the tree. Awareness without naming is a powerful experience that enables a leader to grasp the entire context of a thing, a thought, or an idea.

In detached awareness there is less and less thinking and more and more awareness. The experience is like uncoiling a knot of thoughts and freeing the thread of awareness. This awareness is known as *sakshi*, witness in Sanskrit. The same energy that was being consumed by chaotic thoughts is now fully available to the witness. The witness is alert and active but not involved in thoughts. The *sakshi* can be found by all of us in the silent gap between two thoughts.

Like the swan that dwells in the water and yet does not become drenched, the *sakshi* dwells among thoughts without being swamped by them. The discipline involved in this process is known in Buddhist *vipassana* meditation as "bare attention." In bare attention leaders come to realize that they merely have thoughts, they are not their thoughts—they are something more than the thoughts. By the law of detached awareness, thinkers spontaneously slip into the gap between two thoughts like a deep-sea diver. Thus they enter another plane of consciousness. Here the sea of consciousness does not present the noisy surface of thoughts but the composed silence of pure awareness. The greater the detachment of leaders from their thoughts, the greater is their access to pure awareness.

This search for pure awareness brings us to the third law of conscious leadership, the *law of transcendence*. This law automatically follows the law of detached awareness. A scientist looking for evidence of truth under a microscope is a detached observer. The keener his observation, the closer he comes to the truth behind the observed form or phenomenon. A time comes when the observation is so pure that the scientist eventually zeroes in on the truth. In this act, the observer, the thing observed, and the process of observation are united in one experience. This is the experience of transcendence.

In detached observation leaders are scientists who relate to the world of the actual. In transcendence, leaders are like the visionary who relates to the world of the possible. The dividing line between the actual and the possible is the intangible thing we call *vision*. The actual is the world of facts—it is a world that we can act upon through our senses. The possible is the world of truth. Truth is an invisible phenomenon that cannot be captured by facts; it can only be envisioned and realized by the Self.

In organizations I often hear the phrase *reality check* in the context of managerial leadership. The elaborate paraphernalia of market surveys and feedback from customers constitute some of the instruments of reality check in organizations. Do they check reality, or do they merely affirm what is actual? The actual is what can be seen, quantified, and acted upon immediately. The real is much greater than the actual. The acorn is an actuality—the reality is the giant oak sleeping as a possibility within the acorn. The acorn in actual terms is a small thing, but in real terms it is synonymous with life itself. By means of the law of transcendence alone can the actual be transformed into the real.

Transcendence is taking place every moment in our lives. We transcend time by bringing back memories of past events. Time fast forwards itself when we find ourselves in great company. We transcend space when we forget where we are in the midst of absorbing work. We transcend our physical limitations in our peak performance or when we are faced with great danger. Our egos are transcended when we are deeply in love. Each of these acts of transcendence puts us in touch with a greater reality in ourselves.

The law of transcendence is nothing but transformation of life energy from one form to another. Sometimes we refer to transcendence with a taboo word: *death*. Death is not the end of life as it is commonly believed; it is merely transcendence of life's energy from one form to another. Death in the world of Nature is always a precursor to new life, just as winter is a precursor to spring. Death gives Nature an opportunity to evolve to a new reality. Not only the mystic but also the physicist looks at death as a mere illusion wrought by change of form. One is reminded here again of Einstein's comment on the death of his friend, "This death signifies nothing. For us believing physicists the distinction between past, present and future is only an illusion, even if a stubborn one."

Nature enacts the drama of transcendence in its eternal cycle of birth, evolution, and dissolution. A seed transcends the limitation of its form by opening itself up to the receptive energy of the soil. The seed contains within it the script of a plant's life, but this life cannot manifest itself until the seed decides to die in its present form. As the plant begins to develop from a seed, it soon confronts the limits of its growth. After a while, the plant realizes that it cannot grow up anymore, it can only grow old and perish.

Before it withers away, the intelligence inherent within a fully grown plant prompts it to transcend the reality of its present form and produce a flower. The flower blooms from a bud and assumes a new form. But the flower knows that it must transcend before it withers away. So the flower transcends its form by producing fragrance. This fragrance, in turn, transcends the limitations of space by spreading far and wide. Bees are attracted to the fragrance and pollinate the flower. The flower becomes many seeds. So the single seed that obeyed the law of transcendence is now a part of the continuity of life—from a finite seed it becomes an infinite possibility.

Leadership is a conscious process of discovering and nurturing infinite possibilities in a human being. By not allowing any self-imposed limitation on their own transcendental reality, leaders spontaneously allow followers to transcend themselves, to rise to their individual potential, to exceed the limits of their capability, and to achieve peak performance. Mark Twain once said, "Keep away from people who try to belittle your ambitions. Small people always do that, but the really great make you feel that you, too, can somehow become great."

We can practice the law of transcendence by progressively letting go our urge to hold onto things, objects, addictions, and our urge to be important or powerful. Letting go does not in any way diminish ourselves, it does not make us less influential or less powerful. On the contrary it extends our human capacity for action in infinite ways. When we let go, we in fact let God. We let the intelligence of pure consciousness manifest in us and through us. Mother Teresa described this as "the path of total surrender."

BREATH: THE BRIDGE TO TRANSCENDENCE

Our breath is a bridge to our transcendental reality. Breathing is much more than the physiologic act known as respiration. It is a subtle process that links ourselves with our vast, limitless existence. Simply speaking, our breathing makes us really and truly existential! With every inhalation we breathe in several million atoms of the universe. With every exhalation we breathe out millions of bits of ourselves to the universe. Try this experiment: hold your breath for one minute. You will experience how it feels to lose contact with life. If you can't breathe freely, your existential Self becomes a prisoner of your own body, and death stares you in the face.

In the ordinary state of our minds, we are hardly ever aware of the fact of our breathing. Only when we focus our consciousness on our breath do we begin to understand its subtle processes. Watch what happens to your breathing when you are angry. Your breath becomes more and more shallow; your chest heaves, and your nostrils flare to accommodate as much air as possible. As the normal pattern of your breathing is disrupted, you are thrown off balance, both mentally and physiologically. All our emotional experiences are intimately linked with the way we breathe. Proper management of breath constitutes the fine art of living in harmony with existence.

India's classical wisdom and the science of Yoga, systematically described by Rishi Patanjali around 200 B.C., emphasizes *prayanama*, or the control of bioenergy through disciplined respiratory action. *Pranayama* restores balance to our normally chaotic breathing and brings about a soothing rhythm in our stressful, mechanical lives. By focusing awareness on our inhalations and exhalations, we begin to respond to the mystery of existence.

The simplest of breathing exercises can be practiced through breathing in and breathing out with awareness. While you breathe out, say to yourself mentally, "With each out-breath I go out to the world." And while you breathe in, tell yourself, "With each in-breath I come back to myself." This rhythm of going out and coming in is one of the most fundamental rhythms of life. Going out implies exteriorization of energy. Coming in is the process of interiorization of the same energy. Human life is a pulsation of energy that oscillates between exteriorized and interiorized modes of consciousness. The whole of Nature responds to this rhythm of rest and activity.

The ancient masters of India recognized that breath is not an inorganic matter but an organic entity that integrates the functioning of diverse elements of life. They realized that *prana*, or vital breath, is the basic unit of energy that perpetuates life. According to them, this fundamental energy expresses itself in five primary life currents. These are *prana* (outgoing breath), *apana* (incoming breath), *vyana* (retained breath), *udana* (ascending breath), and *samana* (equalizing breath). *Pranayama* is the ancient discipline of regulating these life currents for effective living.

When we look at the manyfold functions performed by our breathing process, we begin to appreciate why the ancients were so concerned with developing the science of breathing. They judged the value of breath by the remarkable effects that disciplined breathing produced. First they noticed that breathing in a certain manner could regulate body heat. Tibetan masters were able to withstand the chills of the Himalayas in their bare bodies by means of *samana*, that is, by equalizing their body temperature. Then they noticed that by means of disciplining *udana*, or upcoming breath, they could achieve mastery over speech and communication. Even the so-called involuntary functions of the body, such as heartbeat, could be regulated by means of disciplined breathing.

Mere attention to our breathing allows us to unravel the many secrets about our bodies and minds. The ancient Indian masters discovered that the human body had three different dimensions: the gross body, the subtle body, and the causal body. The gross body is concerned with basic physical functions, the subtle body is the seat of mental and emotional functions, and the causal body is the source of consciousness.

By inhabiting our gross body alone, we live in a partial and fragmented world. Here we are like the owner of a multistoried mansion who lives on only one floor of the house. The connecting link between body and the subtle body or the mental body is being discovered today in medical research. The ancients knew several thousand years ago about the integral existence of the body-mind-consciousness axis that constitutes the human being. More important, they knew that the way to gain access to the multidimensional nature of our being is through conscious breathing.

I shall now take you through a three-step breathing exercise that is an integral feature of my leadership workshops. This exercise is drawn from the classical yoga-psychology of India, to which I was initiated by my teacher. I have modified the lessons I have learned myself to make them simpler. These three steps when practiced regularly for 15 minutes twice a day will enable you to understand and activate the power of the three laws of conscious leadership in your daily life. This exercise initially appears to be a tedious technique. Once you have overcome the boredom of doing it routinely, however, you will realize, as I myself have done, that it is a spontaneous and joyful state in which to be.

Step 1: Experiencing the Law of Complete Concentration

Sit comfortably on a chair with your feet firmly grounded on the floor. Do not assume a sloppy or a stiff posture. Balance yourself on your chair comfortably enough so that you can stay that way for ten to fifteen minutes. It helps if the backbone, the neck, and the head fall in a straight line as you sit.

Close your eyes and remain alert to your body. Slowly focus your attention on your breath. With eyes closed be fully aware as you breathe in and breathe out. Remain attentive, for not more than a couple of seconds, to the silent gap between breathing in and breathing out. Do not hold your breath at any point.

As you breath consciously and deeply about fifteen times, you see a wonderful thing happening. Your mind automatically becomes concentrated, and your breath assumes a soothing rhythm. This is the experience of the law of complete concentration.

Step 2: Experiencing the Law of Detached Awareness

Already concentrated in body and mind through conscious breathing, with your eyes closed shift your attention from your breath to your thoughts. This time do not concentrate. Just be gently alert to the steady stream of thoughts in your brain space. You may visualize that your thoughts pass like busy traffic on a road or, better still, like clouds in a sky. Do not be attached to your thoughts, just be a witness. Look for the gap between your thoughts. Never mind if your attention strays, just bring it back with gentle persuasion. Remind yourself that you are not your thoughts—you are just watching them.

Your thoughts slowly diminish in number. As you detach yourself more and more from your thoughts, you grow in awareness. This awareness is what is described earlier as *sakshi*. At this stage your breathing automatically becomes slower, and you become ready to experience transcendence.

Step 3: Experiencing the Law of Transcendence With your eyes closed, take your awareness farther up to the top of your head. Do not concentrate. Completely relax your attention. Visualize that you are gently opening up at the top of your head as the petals of a flower unfold one by one to receive the light of the sun. This opening up is only a visual metaphor to enable your psychosomatic structure to experience a progressive sense of transcendence. As you visualize the opening of a flower and experience the release of its fragrance in the air, you are psychologically transported to a realm of pure light and consciousness. There is no concentration here, no urge to attach or detach—it is an experiment in letting go.

When this experiment reaches a peak, your entire being feels united in body, mind, and senses to one integral experience. Your breathing almost comes to a standstill at this stage. Transcendence is nothing but this realization of your unity with yourself and your environment.

The closing of this exercise is as important as the entire exercise. At the end of transcendence, it is importance to stay with yourself with eyes closed for a couple of minutes. Abrupt closure is likely to ruffle your nervous system. The exercise yields best results when done in small groups, preferably with a guide. However, individuals by themselves can experiment with the three laws of consciousness to understand how disciplined breathing can alter the reality of oneself.

NATURE'S WORK: INERTIA, DYNAMISM, AND AWARENESS

Nature's work is an exquisite synthesis of inertia, dynamism, and awareness. These are the three fundamental modes of expression in Nature. They are three processes that can be seen at work in both the physical and the psychological universe. Inertia is the state of passivity—it is the seed form of a physical or psychologic action. In inertia life is involved inwardly before it can evolve outwardly. Dynamism, the second aspect, is the movement from nonaction to action and from passivity to passion. It is the stage of growth and evolution of form and phenomena. Awareness, the third process, represents another dimension of evolution—the evolution of consciousness. Awareness is not so much growth in the physical realm as it is growth in the psychological realm.

The mineral world represents inertia. Rocks remain the same for millions of years—the change in them is too slow to be detected with our conventional senses. The plant kingdom represents a gradual movement from inertia to dynamism. Plants are capable of rapid growth, but they still are rooted in one place. Their dynamism is static. Animal life, on the other hand, is more dynamic. Animals can change locations and maneuver their universe.

The third quality of Nature, awareness, is something that is largely dormant in plants and present in a very rudimentary stage in the animal kingdom. In human beings, we see the first real evidence of self-awareness. The power of conscious thought and action in the human universe comes from this self-awareness. To be completely self-aware is the highest expression of human evolution.

Nature is not a fixed position but a disposition. It is forever trying to evolve in a certain direction. Human Nature is an accumulation of several dispositions or qualities. Inertia, which is a quality of the most primitive forms of life on earth, is embedded in human nature as laziness, indolence, and stagnation. It is antithetical to movement. Inertia is not necessarily dysfunctional, however, because it helps to conserve energy. A piece of land in which nothing is grown for a long time regains its fertility through inertia.

The quality of dynamism, which is a visible feature of Nature's personality, lends impetus to action. Dynamism is the active principle behind regeneration in Nature. In the physical sense, it is the opposite movement of inertia. Whereas inertia is the force of preservation, dynamism is the agent of change. Human nature, which is dominated by dynamism, gives birth to action-persons. Cultures and countries that have a preponderance of dynamic men and women demonstrate great affluence—glittering cities, huge industries, and technology-driven modes of living. Despite all its advantages, however, dynamism can be dysfunctional if it is not accompanied by awareness. Dynamism without awareness is short-lived and fated to self-destruction. The Roman civilization, which flourished on the wings of dynamic hedonism, collapsed like a house of cards in the absence of illuminated leadership.

How does dynamism evolve into the quality of awareness? This is one of the most remarkable secrets of Nature. The ancient masters of India understood that Nature, including human nature, evolves along two paradoxic paths. One is the path of *pravritti*, in which Nature exteriorizes its energy and bursts out in a riot of forms and shapes and colors. In the psychological universe of human beings, *pravritti* carves out the path of desire and ambition.

The second way of Nature is the way of *nivritti*. It is the interiorized and inward-looking energy in Nature. On this path Nature hibernates, arrests growth, and pulls inward the energy that would otherwise be frittered away in outward expression.

In the psychological sense, *nivritti* represents the force of introspection and mindfulness. When the outgoing dynamism of Nature is arrested temporarily by *nivritti*, the same dynamic energy curves back into itself and evolves into a power of greater subtlety. This energy assumes the quality of illumination. Just as an iron bar heated to a high temperature concentrates its heat energy into light, the energy of dynamism when sufficiently concentrated assumes the quality of illumination.

Awareness, or illumination, which is the third basic component in the evolution of a human being, marks the difference between the subhuman and animal aspects of human beings and their higher Nature. With the dawning of awareness, a human being aspires to the higher strata of Nature's evolution. Intuition begins to function, and the person begins to manifest a certain clarity of vision and empathy for all living forms on earth. Illumination bestows a purposive direction to dynamism and infuses inertia with a positive role for stabilizing the order of Nature.

In Nature the principle and process of leadership work together. The process is the visible relation between various aspects of Nature, and the principle is the underlying law that keeps these processes in order. Inertia, dynamism, and awareness are principles as well as processes. They determine in what direction life will evolve in Nature and how it will do so.

Human beings have assumed leadership among all other species in Nature's kingdom by obeying the evolutionary principle of awareness. This has given them an edge over the dynamism of animal life and the inertia of the plant kingdom. At the same time, the human species is an unfinished process of Nature. Human life is still in the process of evolution toward greater designs of Nature. This evolution is a progressive expansion and unfoldment of consciousness.

A conscious leader makes creative use of the principles as well as the processes of inertia, dynamism, and awareness. Rajat Gupta, chief executive officer of McKinsey, allows some problems to lie undecided because he is conscious that a certain amount of inertia is more useful in solving a problem than is premature and aggressive action. He said, "I tend to let things sort themselves out. Nine problems out of ten go away if you don't address them. You have to deal with the tenth. I often don't address things until I have too."

The secret of right action is to allow action to unfold at the right time rather than force it ahead of its time. A wise leader can hold dynamism in check to gain illumination. Lao-tzu described the essence of this in these wonderful lines: "Whosoever practices non-action, occupies himself with not being occupied, finds taste in what does not taste: he sees the great in the small and the much in the little" (Wilhelm and Oswald, 1995).

NATURE'S CYCLE: A TRYST WITH TIME

> Nature never makes haste; her systems revolve at an even pace. The buds swell imperceptibly, without hurry or confusion, as though the short spring days were an eternity. Why, then, should man hasten as if anything less than eternity were allotted for the least deed.
>
> . . . HENRY DAVID THOREAU (Volkman, 1960)

Nature is a perfect example of the art of waiting. It takes the evolutionary impulse of Nature several thousand years to perfect the shape of a single flower. When we look at natural processes, we realize that there is a certain wisdom implicit in the paradox: faster is slower. How often do we act against the laws of Nature only to realize that we have to spend much greater effort to clean up our mess? In many cultures, patience is misunderstood as plain laziness. As a matter of fact, there is a conscious energy involved in patience that provides impetus toward right action at the right time. Nature demonstrates this day after day.

Only human beings seem to have problems in managing time. No other species on earth apparently suffers from this problem peculiar to our industrial civilization. To me, the problem of time appears to have emerged with the invention of the clock. The clock is the progenitor of chronologic time. Although it serves a very useful purpose in standardizing time around the world, the clock creates a fictitious notion of time as irreversible, uniform, and linear movement of energy.

In Nature, time is never linear, it is cyclical. The laws of Nature clearly tell us that time is not irreversible either. We see the reversal of time in our psychological universe in the form memory of past events. From the memory of physical Nature, seasons come back year after year, crops grow, the sun rises and sets, and planets go round and round in their orbits.

All ancient civilizations considered time not as an impersonal chronologic mechanism measured with a clock but as a living entity that is born, lives, and dies like a human being. In India the word for time is *kala*, which also means death. In the ancient civilizations of South America there is evidence of the worship of time as a living force. There was a good time and a bad time, an auspicious time and an inauspicious one. The people lived in time as they lived in space, avoiding the pitfalls, and setting foot on the right time as if it were firm ground.

We had laughed away the superstitious beliefs of the ancients until Albert Einstein proved that time, like space, is a relative phenomenon. Because of Einstein we have come to realize that time is not merely determined by the clock but is manufactured by the consciousness. Said Einstein, "Sit with your hand on a hot stove for a minute—it would seem like an hour." This renewal of perception of time as a relative phenomenon has taken us back to the wisdom of the ancients who perceived time as a relative quality rather than an absolute quantity.

In defiance of the modern perception of time as a chronologic journey, it may be said that time is not a one-way public thoroughfare, it is also a private apartment. I am talking here about personal time. In the context of space, what we see depends on where we sit. In the context of time, our perspective on time influences how we process time in our consciousness. When our awareness has a chance to expand in time, as when we are in love, time moves at dizzying speed. When our awareness is constricted in a certain time, as when we are doing an unpleasant chore, time stands like a burden on our backs.

Apart from chronologic time, which is unidirectional, there is biologic and psychological time, which are nonlinear and multidimensional. Chronologic time emerges from fragmentation of time into past, present, and future. In this kind of time, the present is always referred to in terms of the past or the future. It is as if the present is nonexistent. A look at the movement of the hands of a mechanical watch reveals that this movement is not smooth but is jerky. The hands jump from the past to the future, bypassing the moment. This linear movement of chronologic time in fits and starts speeds up our psychological clocks. As a result, we are never present in the moment and forever present in the fictitious past or the imaginary future.

This progressive inability to live in the moment, in the here and now of reality, divorces us from reality. We live in the conceptual time of the clock rather than the real time of our biologic and psychological universe. The stress syndrome that pervades modern organizations stems from the fact that in response to external time pressures, our internal clocks run counter to our natural rhythms. The rhythms of our heartbeats, respirations, and hormonal secretions are upset by the mechanical rhythms of machines and work schedules. The inexorable hands of the clock and the sense of vanishing time grip our awareness as we inch toward our self-created deadlines.

Living in chronologic time alone confines us to a closed system in which we conceptualize the irreversible flow of life along with time. This perception of the running down of the self along with time depletes our energy and produces in us fear of time going by. This fear not only is unnerving but also creates great psychological energy leakage. The only way to reverse this tide of time is to live in the present, in the here and now.

Nature teaches us to live in the here and now. The butterfly lives from moment to moment, yet has time enough. The dew drop sits for seconds on a blade of grass, yet it does not panic. The violets and the May flowers gently open to receive the summer's inscriptions, and they never seem to hurry. The busy bee never suffers from stress. All of Nature demonstrates to us the wonderful secret of managing time without being managed by it.

Nature lives in a simultaneous world of time and of time-lessness. All changes in the natural world belong to time. Behind the process of these changes is the principle of continuity, which is changeless and timeless. The process makes sense only in relation to the principle. The principle is the benchmark.

Conscious leaders work in time but live in the world of the timeless. Their lives serve as glorious links between their predecessors and the unborn generations of tomorrow. The actions of conscious leaders are prompted not so much by the pressing needs of their own survival but by the higher aspirations of life to perpetuate itself. Gandhi bore testimony to the timeless aspirations of a conscious leader as follows (Fischer, 1962):

> "[While] everything around me is ever changing, ever dying, there is underlying all that change a living power that is change-less, that holds all together, that creates dissolves and recreates... For I can see in the midst of death life persists, in the midst of untruth truth persists, in the midst of darkness light persists.
>
> . . . MOHANDAS K. GANDHI

NATURE'S MANUSCRIPT: MEDITATIONS FOR LEADERS

The Freedom of the Sky

> The soil in return for service keeps the tree tied to her, the sky asks nothing and leaves it free.
>
> . . . RABINDRANATH TAGORE, *Fireflies*, 1955

A tired traveler, returning home after a grueling day's work, encounters a bleak, soulless city. The sun has slipped unceremoniously behind skyscrapers. Columns of streetlights have begun to wink eerily through a heavy smog. The din of traffic drowns the voice of a bird perched on an electric wire. The traveler feels the agony of having to make a living in this cage-like city.

The traveler looks heavenward for relief only to discover that even God's sky has been blotted out by giant billboards. Yet the sky remains for many of us a constant reminder that we are essentially free beings and dwellers of the infinite. The endless blue we see above us defies the geometry of the cityscape. The sky is an open invitation to us to experience the freedom of the formless.

Freedom is a state of consciousness. It does not lie outside us. Rather our search to be free is an inward quest—a journey within to liberate ourselves from our self-created prisons. Stone walls, the poet Lovelace said, do not a prison make; our mental blocks do. The iron bars of our fears and prejudices hold us in psychological bondage. They do not allow us to taste freedom that is our birth right. The Upanishads say that the prime goal of human beings is attainment of freedom or *moksha*, the Buddhists call this *nirvana*, or the extinction of bondage.

The infinite grace that shapes the majesty of the sky also embraces us. Every time we contemplate the sky, we are in touch with our omnipresence. The vast sky is not apart from us but is only a part of us and proclaims in the majestic language of the stars the message of our own freedom.

Tibetan lamas often teach their disciples to meditate on the sky. The disciples are advised to lie flat on their backs, preferably in the open, to get a clear view of the sky. Alternatively, they are advised to look up to the sky while standing or sitting in a comfortable position. One has to make sure that the vision is not obstructed by other objects in sight. As one contemplates the vast blue of the sky, the consciousness expands progressively. After some time, the limiting notions of one's body and mental tensions ease out. Slowly one begins to experience the joy and freedom of merging with the source of pure consciousness.

The Message of the Mountains

> To see the greatness of a mountain, one must keep one's distance.
> . . . ANGARIKA GOVINDA

Mountains teach us the art of detachment. They inspire us to transcend the mundane and rise in aspiration and in strength to all that is highest and purest in the world. The mountain listens silently to the magnificent music of the wind as it sweeps across its rocky face. Unruffled by the lashing of rains and the rumblings of thunder, the mountains stand as the earth's most enduring monuments.

Mountains have posed constant challenge to human motivation. Pilgrims, trekkers, tourists, and climbers have looked on mountains as symbols of their aspirations. The lure of the hills is the lure of the unknown and the unconquered aspects of our own selves. There is a mountain in our psyche that corresponds to that in physical Nature—the only difference between them is a difference in scale and perspective.

The snow-capped hills not only allow us to perform feats of endurance but also fill us with a feeling of wonder and a sense of the sacred. One has to abandon many of the bodily comforts in the process of climbing a mountain. In renunciation of our attachment to these comforts of the plains, we are in touch with a consciousness of the sacred. Mount Kailas in India, the summit of Mount Fuji in Japan, the T'ai Shan in China all have been revered as sacred places in the consciousness of the world's most enduring civilizations.

The transfiguration of Jesus and his transformation into a reality take place on a mountain. Muhammad hears the revelations of Allah in a cave in Mount Hira on the outskirts of Mecca. The sages of the Himalayas have found timeless truths in the bosom of the mountain. Physically and symbolically, the mountains have transported human beings of all ages to reflective states of consciousness.

In the earth-defying silence of the mountain we encounter a vertical pull of a higher state of consciousness. Physical altitude triggers a psychic journey into a higher realm. Those of us who have meditated deeply on the mountain intuitively know this. Mountain climbing is a rigorous physical act. A climber learns great lessons about reaching goals in the process of climbing. Rene Daumal gave us this remarkable piece of wisdom about mountain climbing that has great significance for our pilgrimage of leadership:

> Keep your eye fixed on the way to the top, but don't forget to look right in front of you. The last step depends on the first. Don't think you are there just because you see the summit. Watch your footing, be sure of the next step, but don't let that distract you from the highest goal. The first step depends on the last.
>
> . . . RENE DAUMAL, "Mount Analogue,"
> quoted in *Parabola*, November 1988

Lessons from a Garden

> Raise the stone, and there thou shalt find me, cleave the wood and there am I.
>
> . . . THE SAYINGS OF JESUS, *Oxyrhynchus Papyri*, Third century

If you spend some time inside a Japanese garden, you will see a miniature landscape of the human mind. You may call it the mindscape. You will see flowers, bushes, shrubs, and an assortment of foliage the names of which you may not know. For me a garden has often seemed like a fascinating contour of the inner world of a human being.

The solid rocks are like the fortresses of values that are deeply entrenched in the heart and give us a sense of stability in an everchanging world. The running water, sparkling in the sun, is the clear stream of reason that winds its way through the dense mass of ignorance. The soft, moist soil is a fertile bed of emotion on which grows a riot of colors and forms—the peaceful white lily, the shy rose, and the flamboyant marigold.

The pine tree meditates, sage-like, on the edge of the garden. Ants crawl on the earth like a tenacious chain of thoughts. If you divert their path by flicking a stone, they regroup themselves again—such is their nature. The soft, white sands bear the footprints of a squirrel just as our scattered mind picks up imprints of any stray sight or sound.

The wind leaves its graffiti like the impressions of our senses on everything in the garden. It touches the silken surface of the leaves, murmurs through dried leaves, and inscribes its message on the sand.

As I sat reflecting upon the garden, a sudden insight came to me: if our mind is like a garden, then it must be the creation of a gardener who is a master of this unique conception. The garden must have come from the awareness of the gardener—the sense of tension and harmony, the contrast and coherence in its many forms—all these must have had their source in the mind of the gardener. The landscape outside therefore is just a projection of the landscape inside.

I conjectured that our own minds, like the garden, are perhaps a projection of a higher Mind. This mind of ours is only a finite expression of a higher intelligence, which conceived us. Although we are thinking beings ourselves, it is also possible that we are being thought of by a larger entity. Are we therefore not connected to this higher Self just as the garden is integrally connected with the gardener? Perhaps the only way to be in touch with the higher mind is to suspend the boundaries of our limited minds and dissolve ourselves into the unlimited, as the garden outside and the garden inside merge in the mind of the gardener. A prayer came to my heart in the middle of all these thoughts:

> Let me be just one song,
> A universe of thought, feeling and action.
> Let me touch the entire world
> Just as sun's rays caress the darkest planet.
> Let me be as humble as a blade of grass
> And as tolerant as a tree,
> Which gives shade even the one
> Who prepares to cut it down.

Self-Organizing Universe We often talk about our self in the environment. I would like to modify that statement in the light of my own experience. I would like to say that one's self *is* the environment. This would result in a crisis of perception among those of us who are accustomed to defining the outer limit of self as the beginning of the environment. If, however, we define our environment not in terms of objects but simply as a set of relationships, it becomes clear that nothing can be part of our environment if it is not related to our selves. Whatever is related to our selves becomes part of us.

Even the farthest star that we can see in our galaxy has a certain relation with us. The moment our eyes see the star, the retinas of the eyes enter into a direct relation with the star. The light of the star reflects on our eyes. The star becomes as much a part of our eyes as we become a part of the star. If you meditate on this deeply, you will know that this is absolutely true.

We live not in a world of objects but in a universe of relationships. Even the so-called objects are not quite objects; they are relationships. The house in which you live is not an object, it is a relationship among brick, wood, sand, cement, and the hand that built it. The car you drive in is a relationship among its various mechanical and electronic parts, the fuel, and the driver. You yourself are a bundle of relationships and a bridge between your ancestors and your posterity.

The unique process that makes a relational world viable is the process of self-organization. A caterpillar contains a set of relationships that can reorganize themselves and become a butterfly. A piece of coal is a relationship between several atoms of carbon. When this relationship changes, the same carbon atoms combine to form a diamond. A lump of clay with a foul smell becomes, through a change in relationships between its atoms, the fragrance of a beautiful flower. Conscious leaders see a butterfly within a caterpillar, diamond within coal, and a flower in a piece of clay simply because they are aware of the power of a self-organizing universe.

The universe of self-organization is finite in its expression and infinite in its principle. It is finite in the sense that it revolves around a specific identity from which the organization flows. But the principle of relatedness within an organization is universal and goes beyond a specific identity. An organization builds its commercial identity on a set of core products or businesses. The self-organizing corporation, however, goes beyond the products themselves in search of new relationships between products and people. Sony had its commercial identity in the business of tape recorders and headphones. Yet the power of Self-organization within Sony built a new product based on the relationship between a tape recorder and a headphone—the Walkman. The Walkman was the beginning of a new relationship between Sony and its customers. The self-organizing capability of computer technology has built bridges of relationships between computers and communication, computers and transportation, computers and management, and so on.

If we look intimately into the nature of our own Selves, we see their remarkable capacity to organize themselves. The human embryo, cut off from the outside world for nine months, organizes itself in relation to its core identity. When this embryo emerges to the light of the sun, it is a formidable entity capable of living a life of immense complexity.

Self-organization is the law of being of all sentient life in our universe. The ancient Indian masters realized this clearly when they were in search of what they described as *dharma*. *Dharma* is the emergent property of all living forms that enables them to relate to their environment. *Dharma* is not apparent because it is inherent not in objects but in relationships. The seed can express its *dharma* only in relation to the soil. The fish can express it only in relation to water. The power and knowledge of self-organization are implicit in the *dharma* of all life forms. It is only within the framework of relationships that the process of self-organization becomes explicit.

Conscious leaders are not in search of power or knowledge. They are simply in search of Self. In this search they realize that the root of all power and knowledge lies deep within the *dharma* of the Self. The moment one discovers one's *dharma*, she spontaneously discovers her unique relationship with the world. She is like the bird that with the first flutter of its wings discovers its relationship with the air. The leader's power to fly lies in this relationship.

Each one us of in leadership positions is asking the same question in different languages and in different contexts. The question is: how can I be my very best? Many of us realize that we can be our very best when we are truly related to ourselves, to our own *dharma*. In that relationship alone can we find our relatedness to the world at large.

Jesus said: Become passers-by.
. . . The Gospel According to
Thomas, Log. 42

9

Epilogue: The Sacred Path of Leadership

VIRTUOUS REALITY: THE LEADERSHIP PILGRIMAGE

A pilgrimage is different from all other kind of journey. In a pilgrimage destination lies within us. The true pilgrimage is as much a journey in space and time as it is a journey in consciousness. Leadership is a pilgrimage of consciousness. Leaders in all fields of endeavor serve as perspective providers who give direction to life. They see life not only in the context of the actual but also from the vantage point of the possible.

In this leaders are pioneers of the world. They discover new faces of reality. They travel to unknown spaces, and after they have seen what was hitherto unseen, cry out: "Come on folks! Here is a new land." The followers know it is perfectly safe to undertake the journey, because the leader has already undertaken it before them. They start their journey with full faith in the leader. Both the leader and the follower are travelers on the same path; the only difference is that the leader not only has excellent road sense but also has a sense of destination.

To undertake a pilgrimage, we must first have faith in the destination. In this case, the ultimate destination, as I have already said, is the Self. Faith is something that is best described by the expression *virtuous reality*. Faith has its own kind of logic and its own reality. Otherwise how can you explain the fact that the largest and most enduring organizations of the world are all based on faith? It is the search for constant truths about ourselves that inspires us to move in the realm of faith. In faith we obey our own essence.

The second requirement for this leadership pilgrimage is the right kind of discipline. One has to discover, through trial and error, the right effort that enables one to negotiate the obstacles that arise. The pilgrim's path is beset with hardships and temptations at every turn. It is easy to give up in hardships and give in to the temptation of turning away from one's path. The journey of self-conquest and self-transcendence is a slow one. It demands patience and perseverance. The light comes gently, but it surely comes.

The third dimension is the presence of a master. A master is simply a presence. A master is like the light of the lamp in whose presence we acquire clarity and luminosity in our journey. Masters are not interested in imparting information. Their interest is in transformation. They themselves are transformed beings; therefore they can bring about transformation in others. You can light many lamps from one source. And when you place many lamps in one room, they give the same light. It is impossible to differentiate the light of one lamp from that of another. At the end of the journey, the master and the disciple, the leader and the led become part of that one light—the light of consciousness.

In these last few pages I present brief profiles of six leaders of the world who have led us by the light of their consciousness. They represent a tradition of the search for the sacred. Their pilgrimages toward self-mastery were nothing but heroic. In the course of their journeys they transformed themselves and millions of others. They organized masses into enduring institutions.

Buddha, Gandhi, Mother Teresa, Lao-tzu, Confucius, and Vive-kananda all have left their indelible footprints on civilization.

At the turn of the century the very sustainability of the earth-system has reached crisis proportions. It sounds like a cliché to talk about environmental havoc, utter mismanagement of the world's natural resources, and the specter of hunger and poverty in the middle of plenty. To me the greatest paradox is that we are such a rich world of poor people. Our poverty is the poverty of indifference, callousness, and lack of attention in addressing our self-created problems.

The real crisis that faces us today is the crisis of consciousness. Those of us who hold positions of power and privilege in business, politics, academics, sports, medicine, and religious institutions have simply to wake up and address this crisis. Leading consciously is not an esoteric formula for personal salvation—it is an urgent and emergent need for our own survival as a civilization. The leaders of tomorrow have a debt to their destiny to fulfill the dreams of the likes of Buddha, Gandhi, and Mother Teresa. To the conscious leaders of the next century, I dedicate the legacy of our great masters.

BUDDHA: I AM JUST AWAKE

Buddha means *the awakened one*. When people, puzzled by his identity, asked Buddha: "Who are you? Are you a man? A God? Or an Angel?" Buddha said, "I am just awake." Born around 563 B.C., Buddha abandoned a princely life to end human suffering. Buddhism was born as a religion of infinite compassion. Buddha's message set on fire the entire Indian subcontinent and spread to China, Tibet, Japan, and eventually the entire world. Buddha's message was direct, simple, and practical. He said: "What have I explained? I have explained the cause of suffering, and the destruction of suffering, and the path that leads to the destruction of suffering. For this is useful" (Smith, 1991).

Buddha's leadership was evident not only in the size of his following and the spread of his order but also in the perfection of his discipline. He discovered the *middle path* of leadership, which was the path of perceptive wisdom between the extremes of austerity and indulgence. Buddha demonstrated the virtue of intense self-effort and self-reliance and proclaimed, "Those who, relying upon themselves only, shall not look for assistance to any one besides themselves, it is they who shall reach the top-most height" (Smith, 1991). Buddha's last words to his favorite disciple Ananda were: "Be lamps unto yourselves. Attach your-selves to no external means. Hold fast as a refuge to the Truth. Work out your own salvation with diligence" (Smith, 1991).

BUDDHA

GANDHI: MY LIFE IS MY MESSAGE

Gandhi's entire life was an experiment with Truth. He proclaimed, "Truth is my God. Non-violence is the means of realizing Him" (Radhakrishnan, 1956). On the basis of these two principles alone, this unarmed messiah took on the might of an entire empire and gave freedom to his country. After Buddha, Gandhi was the greatest spiritual force in world history. No leader can describe himself accurately, he can only reveal himself through his actions. This is true of Gandhi. When a journalist asked him for a message for the United States, Gandhi said: "My life is its own message" (Radhakrishnan, 1956).

There was a fundamental integrity between Gandhi's leadership theory and practice. He demonstrated an amazing synchronicity among his speech, thought, and action. Gandhi was an embodiment of the trusteeship principle of leadership. For him a leader was responsible for holding in trust the power that followers gave him. A misuse of this power was for Gandhi a betrayal of trust. Albert Einstein, a contemporary of Gandhi commented:

> The moral influence which he has exercised upon thinking people throughout the civilized world may be far more durable than would appear likely in our present age, with its exaggeration of brute force. . . . We are fortunate and should be grateful that fate has bestowed upon us so luminous a contemporary—a beacon to the generations to come.
>
> . . . SARVEPALLI RADHAKRISHNAN, *Mahatma Gandhi*, 1956

M.K. GANDHI

MOTHER TERESA:
SMALL WORK WITH GREAT LOVE

Mother Teresa is the example of a leader whose power of love triumphed over love of power. Abandoning her career as a school teacher, she responded to the inner call of serving the poorest of poor in the slums of Calcutta. The founder of the Missionaries of Charity, which provides care and service to destitute people across the globe, Mother Teresa was described by the Secretary General of the United Nations as "the most powerful woman of the world."

Mother Teresa's leadership was based on this simple philosophy: small work with great love. She said about her mission, "Our vocation is not the work—the fidelity to humble works is our means to put our love into action." A tireless crusader for the underprivileged of the world, Mother Teresa led countless people on the path of service and love. Reacting to a question about what she felt when people addressed her as a living saint, she said with her characteristic humility:

> You have to be holy in your position as you are, and I have to be holy in the position that God has put me. So it is nothing extraordinary to be holy. Holiness is not the luxury of the few. Holiness is a simple duty for you and for me. We have been created for that.

MOTHER TERESA

LAO-TZU: THE TAO OF LEADERSHIP

"To lead people, walk behind them," said Lao-tzu, China's most revered philosopher and sage (*Tao Te Ching*). Lao-tzu literally means, "the old master." According to the traditions of China, Lao-tzu was born about 604 B.C. A legendary figure, this grand old man of China is said to have written the *Tao Te Ching* (The Way and Its Power) which is the second most translated book in the world after the Bible.

Lao-tzu was a mystic who spent most of his time in quiet contemplation. His life was an embodiment of the eternal and invisible principle that governs the world. According to Lao-tzu, mastery comes from understanding and harmonizing one's life with *Tao* which is the ineffable and spontaneous order of Nature. Leadership, according to Lao-tzu, is a state of consciousness. In the words of Lao-tzu, effective leadership comes from self-awareness and self-conquest: "He who knows other men is discerning; he who knows himself is intelligent. He who overcomes others is strong; he who overcomes himself is mighty" (*Tao Te Ching*).

LAO-TZU

CONFUCIUS: THE MORAL LEADER

Confucius, who lived from 551 to 479 B.C., was a philosopher, teacher, king-maker, and social reformer. At the age of seventy years he said about himself, "At fifteen I began to be seriously interested in study. At thirty I had formed my character. At fifty I knew the will of heaven. At sixty nothing that I heard disturbed me. At seventy I could let my thoughts wander without trespassing the moral law" (Smith, 1991). Confucius single-handedly crafted an ethical, socially oriented philosophy that dominated Chinese civilization for many years. From the *Analects*, which contains the conversations of Confucius, we get the crystallized wisdom of the world's most influential teacher and humanist.

Confucius looked upon the leader as the perfect "gentleman." He said leaders were like "gentlemen never compete." For him leadership was not an outcome of brute force and competitive rivalry but a spontaneous flowering of a moral power. Confucius said: "To find the central clue to our moral being which unites us to the universal order, that indeed is the highest human achievement."

CONFUCIUS

SWAMI VIVEKANANDA: SERVANT LEADERSHIP

"Everyone can play the role of the master but it is very difficult to be a servant," said Swami Vivekananda. He was known as the "cyclonic monk" who after thirty-nine years of life left a legacy of unflinching service and institution building. Born in 1863, Vivekananda was the first living example for the West of the wisdom and spirit of India. Dedicating himself to his Master, Vivekananda founded the order of Ramakrishna Mission, which survives worldwide nearly a hundred years after his death as a testimonial to his sound leadership.

"One must be a servant of servants and must accommodate a thousand minds. There must not be a shade of jealousy or self-ishness, then you are a leader," said Vivekananda about the qualities of servant leadership. He embodied all the three attributes of a servant leader: a purity of purpose, a persever-ance of effort, and a passion for service. Swami Vivekananda said: "He only lives who lives for others. The rest are more dead than alive."

SWAMI VIVEKANANDA

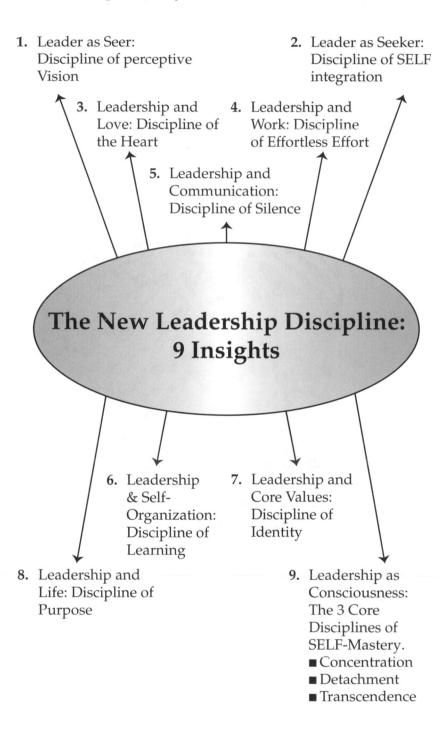

1. Leader as Seer: Discipline of perceptive Vision

2. Leader as Seeker: Discipline of SELF integration

3. Leadership and Love: Discipline of the Heart

4. Leadership and Work: Discipline of Effortless Effort

5. Leadership and Communication: Discipline of Silence

The New Leadership Discipline: 9 Insights

6. Leadership & Self-Organization: Discipline of Learning

7. Leadership and Core Values: Discipline of Identity

8. Leadership and Life: Discipline of Purpose

9. Leadership as Consciousness: The 3 Core Disciplines of SELF-Mastery.
   ■ Concentration
   ■ Detachment
   ■ Transcendence

Shifting Paradigms
of Conscious Leadership

FROM:

- Capability
- Job enrichment
- Quality circles
- Balanced personality
- Intellectual culture
- Strategy
- Leadership
- Virtual reality

TO:

- Copability
- Self-enrichment
- Quality consciousness
- Integrated personality
- Emotional awareness
- Purpose
- Followership
- Virtuous reality

References

PRELUDE

Tagore, Rabindranath. *Gitanjali.* London: Macmillan, 1913.

CHAPTER 1

Barker, Joel Arthur. *Future Edge: Discovering the New Paradigms of Success.* New York: William Morrow, 1992.

Barks, Coleman, trans. *The Essential Rumi.* New York: Harper Collins, 1995.

Bryner, Andy, and Dawna Markova. *An Unused Intelligence: Physical Thinking for 21st Century Leadership.* Berkeley: Conari Press, 1996.

Chopra, Deepak. *Quantum Healing: Exploring the Frontiers of Mind and Body Science.* New York: Bantam Books, 1989.

———. *The Seven Spiritual Laws of Success.* Novato, California: Amber-Allen Publishing and New World Library, 1994.

Greenleaf, Robert K. *Servant Leadership: A Journey into the Nature of Legitimate Power and Greatness.* Mahwah, New Jersey: Paulist Press, 1977.

Guenther, Hebert, and Kawamura Leslie, trans. *Mind in Buddhist Psychology.* Emeryville, California: Dharma Publishing, 1975.

Senge, Peter M. *The Fifth Discipline: The Art and Practice of Learning Organization.* New York: Doubleday, 1990.

Sobel, Jyoti, and Prem Sobel. *The Hierarchy of Minds: A Compilation from the Works of Sri Aurobindo and the Mother.* Pondicherry, India: Sri Aurobindo Ashram Publications Department, 1991.

Yasuo, Yuasa. *The Body, Self Cultivation and Ki-Energy.* New York: State University of New York Press, 1993.

CHAPTER 2

Asimov, Isaac. *The Dialogues of Plato.* Oxford: Clarendon Press, 1953.

———. Words of Science: And the History Behind Them. New York: New American Library, 1959.

———. "Today's Leaders Look to Tomorrow," *Fortune*, 26 March 1990.

Campbell, Joseph. *The Masks of God: Creative Mythology.* New York: Viking, 1968.

Capra, Fritjof. *The Tao of Physics.* Boston: Shambala Publications, 1975.

———. *Uncommon Wisdom.* New York: Simon & Schuster, 1988.

———. *The Web of Life.* New York: Anchor Books, 1996.

Dalai Lama. *The Way of Freedom.* New Delhi: Harper Collins, 1995.

Merell-Wolff, Franklin. *The Philosophy of Consciousness Without an Object.* New York: Julian Press, 1973.

Ranganathananda, Swami. *A Scientific Approach to Religion.* New York: State University of New York Press, 1991.

Sherman, Stratford. "Leadership Can Be Learnt," *Span*, April-May 1996.

Ornstein, Robert E. *The Psychology of Consciousness.* New York: Harcourt Brace Jovanovich, 1977.

Mahadevan, T.M.P. *Talks with Sri Ramana Maharshi.* Madras, India: Sri Ramana Sramam Tiruvannamalai, 1989.

Pyarelal. *Mahatma Gandhi: The Early Phase.* Ahmedabad, India: Navajivan, 1956.

CHAPTER 3

Aurobindo, Sri. *The Message of the Gita.* Pondicherry, India: Sri Aurobindo Ashram, 1977.

Barks, Coleman. *The Essential Rumi.* New York: Harper Collins, 1995.

Boldt, Laurence G. *How to Find the Work You Love.* New York: Arkana, 1993.

Lindbergh, Charles A. *Autobiography of Values.* New York: Harcourt Brace Jovanovich, 1978.

Mother Teresa. *Total Surrender.* Ann Arbor: Servant Publications, 1985.

Sobel, Jyoti, and Prem Sobel. *The Hierarchy of Minds: A Compilation from the works of Sri Aurobindo and the Mother.* Pondicherry, India: Sri Aurobindo Ashram Publications Department, 1991.

Robertson, Ronald. *Globalization: Social Theory and Global Culture.* London: Sage Publications, 1992.

Stark, Eleanor. *The Gift Unopened: A New American Revolution.* Portsmouth, New Hampshire: Peter E. Randall Publisher, 1988.

Wilson, Andrew. *World Scripture: A Comparative Anthology of Sacred Texts.* New Delhi: Motilal Banarsidas, 1993.

CHAPTER 4

Cannon, Walter B. *Wisdom of the Body.* New York: W. W. Norton, 1963.

Fischer, Louis, ed. *The Essential Gandhi.* New York: Vintage Books, 1962.

Jacobi, Jolande, ed. *Parcelsus: Selected Writings.* Princeton: Princeton University Press, 1969.

Krishnamurti, J. *On Learning and Knowledge.* New York: Harper Collins, 1994.

Mother Teresa. *Total Surrender.* Ann Arbor: Servant Publications, 1985.

Remde, Harry. *The Art in a Craft.* Toronto: Traditional Studies Press, 1975.

Renesch, John, ed. *New Traditions in Business.* San Francisco: Sterling and Stone, 1991.

Senge, Peter M. *The Fifth Discipline: The Art and Practice of Learning Organization.* New York: Doubleday, 1990.

Tagore, Rabindranath. *Fireflies.* New York: Macmillan, 1955.

Williams, Charles. *The Place of the Lion.* Grand Rapids: William B. Eerdmans, 1965.

CHAPTER 5

Abram, David. *The Spell of the Sensuous.* New York: Pantheon Books, 1996.

Aurobindo, Sri, and The Mother. *On Self-Perfection.* Pondicherry, India: Sri Aurobindo Ashram, 1973.

————. *Parabola*, August 1983.

Barks, Coleman. *The Essential Rumi.* New York: Harper Collins, 1995.

Krishnamurti, J. *On Learning and Knowledge.* New York: Harper Collins, 1994.

Mahadevan, T.M.P. Talks with Sri Ramana Maharshi. Madras, India: Sri Ramana Sramam Tiruvannamalai, 1989.

Mother Teresa. *Total Surrender.* Ann Arbor: Servant Publications, 1985.

Swarup, Ram. The Word as Revelation. New Delhi: Impex India, 1980.

CHAPTER 6

Chakraborty, S.K. *Management by Values.* New Delhi: Oxford University Press, 1993.

Chan, Wing-sit. *A Source Book in Chinese Philosophy.* Princeton: Princeton University Press, 1963.

Dalai Lama. *The Way To Freedom.* New Delhi: Harper Collins, 1995.

Fischer, Louis, ed. *The Essential Gandhi.* New York: Vintage Books, 1962.

Fukuyama, Francis. *The End of History and the Last Man.* New York, Avon, 1992.

Gibran, Kahlil. *The Prophet.* New York: Alfred A. Knopf, 1970.

Griggs, Lewis Brown, and Lente-Louise Low, eds. *Valuing Diversity: New Tools for a New Reality.* New York: McGraw-Hill, 1995.

Kurien, V. *Managing Socio-Economic Change: The Role of Professionals.* Ahmedabad, India: Indian Institute of Management Publication, 1978.

Pollar, Odette, and Rafael Gonzalez. *Dynamics of Diversity.* California: Crisp Publications, 1994.

Russell, Bertrand. *The Scientific Outlook.* London: George Allen & Unwin, 1931.

Saint-Exupery, Antoine de. *The Little Prince.* New York: Harcourt Brace Jovanovich, 1971.

Senge, Peter M. *The Fifth Discipline: The Art and Practice of Learning Organization.* New York: Doubleday, 1990.

Walsh, James. "Asia's Different Drum," *Time* 14 June 1993.

CHAPTER 7

Chopra, Deepak. *The Path to Love.* New York: Rider Books, 1997.

Gibran, Kahlil. *The Prophet*. New York: Alfred A. Knopf, 1970.

Krishnamurti, J. *On Learning and Knowledge.* New York: Harper Collins, 1994.

Moir, Anne, and David Jessel. *Brainsex.* New York: Dell Publishing, 1989.

Mother Teresa. *Total Surrender.* Ann Arbor: Servant Publications, 1985.

Wilhelm, Richard, and H. G. Oswald, trans. *Lao-tzu.* New York: Penguin Books, 1995.

CHAPTER 8

Daumal, Rene. "Mount Analogue," quoted in *Parabola* November 1988.

Fischer, Louis, ed. *The Essential Gandhi.* New York: Vintage Books, 1962.

Frawley, David. *Wisdom of the Ancient Seers.* Salt Lake City: Passage Press, 1992.

Hughes, Holly, and Mark Weakley. *Meditations on the Earth.* Philadelphia: Running Press, 1994.

Krishnamurti, J. *On Learning and Knowledge.* New York: Harper Collins Publishers, 1994.

Mother Teresa. *Total Surrender.* Ann Arbor: Servant Publications, 1985.

Tagore, Rabindranath. *Fireflies.* New York: Macmillan, 1955.

Volkman, Arthur G. *Thoreau on Man and Nature.* New York: Peter Pauper Press, 1960.

CHAPTER 9

Mother Teresa. *Total Surrender.* Ann Arbor: Servant Publications, 1985.

Radhakrishnan, Sarvepalli. *Mahatma Gandhi.* Bombay: Jaico Publishing, 1956.

Smith, Houston. *The World's Religions.* New York: Harper, 1991.

Butterworth-Heinemann Business Books . . .
for Transforming Business

5th Generation Management: Co-creating Through Virtual Enterprising, Dynamic Teaming, and Knowledge Networking, Revised Edition,
Charles M. Savage, 0-7506-9701-6

After Atlantis: Working, Managing, and Leading in Turbulent Times,
Ned Hamson, 0-7506-9884-5

The Alchemy of Fear: How to Break the Corporate Trance and Create Your Company's Successful Future,
Kay Gilley, 0-7506-9909-4

Beyond Strategic Vision: Effective Corporate Action with Hoshin Planning,
Michael Cowley and Ellen Domb, 0-7506-9843-8

Beyond Time Management: Business with Purpose,
Robert A. Wright, 0-7506-9799-7

The Breakdown of Hierarchy: Communicating in the Evolving Workplace,
Eugene Marlow and Patricia O'Connor Wilson, 0-7056-9746-6

Business and the Feminine Principle: The Untapped Resource,
Carol R. Frenier, 0-7506-9829-2

Choosing the Future: The Power of Strategic Thinking,
Stuart Wells, 0-7506-9876-4

Cultivating Common Ground: Releasing the Power of Relationships at Work,
Daniel S. Hanson, 0-7506-9832-2

Flight of the Phoenix: Soaring to Success in the 21st Century,
John Whiteside and Sandra Egli, 0-7506-9798-9

Getting a Grip on Tomorrow: Your Guide to Survival and Success in the Changed World of Work,
Mike Johnson, 0-7506-9758-X

Innovation Strategy for the Knowledge Economy: The Ken Awakening,
Debra M. Amidon, 0-7506-9841-1

The Intelligence Advantage: Organizing for Complexity,
Michael D. McMaster, 0-7506-9792-X

Intuitive Imagery: A Resource at Work,
John B. Pehrson and Susan E. Mehrtens, 0-7506-9805-5

The Knowledge Evolution: Expanding Organizational Intelligence,
Verna Allee, 0-7506-9842-X

Leadership in a Challenging World: A Sacred Journey,
Barbara Shipka, 0-7506-9750-4

Leading Consciously: A Pilgrimage Toward Self Mastery,
Debashis Chatterjee, 0-7506-9864-0

Leading from the Heart: Choosing Courage over Fear in the Workplace,
Kay Gilley, 0-7506-9835-7

Learning to Read the Signs: Reclaiming Pragmatism in Business,
F. Byron Nahser, 0-7506-9901-9

Leveraging People and Profit: The Hard Work of Soft Management,
Bernard A. Nagle and Perry Pascarella, 0-7506-9961-2

Marketing Plans That Work: Targeting Growth and Profitability,
Malcolm H.B. McDonald and Warren J. Keegan, 0-7506-9828-4

A Place to Shine: Emerging from the Shadows at Work,
Daniel S. Hanson, 0-7506-9738-5

Power Partnering: A Strategy for Business Excellence in the 21st Century,
Sean Gadman, 0-7506-9809-8

Putting Emotional Intelligence to Work: Successful Leadership is More Than IQ,
David Ryback, 0-7506-9956-6

Resources for the Knowledge-Based Economy Series

The Knowledge Economy,
Dale Neef, 0-7506-9936-1

Knowledge Management and Organizational Design,
Paul S. Myers, 0-7506-9749-0

Knowledge Management Tools,
Rudy L. Ruggles, III, 0-7506-9849-7

Knowledge in Organizations,
Laurence Prusak, 0-7506-9718-0

The Strategic Management of Intellectual Capital,
David A. Klein, 0-7506-9850-0

The Rhythm of Business: The Key to Building and Running Successful Companies,
Jeffrey C. Shuman, 0-7506-9991-4

Setting the PACE® in Product Development: A Guide to Product and Cycle-time Excellence,
Michael E. McGrath, 0-7506-9789-X

Time to Take Control: The Impact of Change on Corporate Computer Systems,
Tony Johnson, 0-7506-9863-2

The Transformation of Management,
Mike Davidson, 0-7506-9814-4

What is the Emperor Wearing? Truth-Telling in Business Relationships,
Laurie Weiss, 0-7506-9872-1

Who We Could Be at Work, Revised Edition,
Margaret A. Lulic, 0-7506-9739-3

Working From Your Core: Personal and Corporate Wisdom in a World of Change,
Sharon Seivert, 0-7506-9931-0

To purchase any Butterworth-Heinemann title, please visit your local bookstore or call 1-800-366-2665.

Debashis Chatterjee is an internationally known management thinker, Fulbright scholar, corporate consultant, mystic, and writer. He is a member of the faculty in the behavioral sciences department at the Indian Institute of Management in Lucknow, India. He has lectured and taught at Harvard Graduate School of Business, University of St. Thomas, Tufts University and at the Indian Institute of Management in Calcutta. Chatterjee conducts worldwide leadership and self-management programs for diverse audiences of executives, doctors, scientists, political leaders, and social service workers.

In *Leading Consciously*, Chatterjee brings together his experience as an executive and trainer in Fortune 500 companies such as Ford Motor Company, AT&T, Motorola, and 3M with his spiritual insights gained in the company of holy men and women of India, including Mother Teresa. This work is a unique synthesis of the latest breakthroughs in Western empirical sciences and classical wisdom of the East. An immensely popular speaker on the themes of spirituality and modern management, Chatterjee organizes frequent leadership retreats in India and around the world. He may be reached at: kunurika@iiml.ac.in

For more information on Debashis Chatterjee's workshops on Leadership and Self-Mastery or to contact the author, write to any of the following addresses:

Foundation for Leadership and Human Development
109 Gulliver St.
Milton, MA 02186 U.S.

Mrs. Arundahati Ghosal
130 Desborough Ave.
Highwycombe, Bucks
HP112SQ United Kingdom

Foundation for Leadership and Human Development
28, B.L. Hati Road
Burdwan 713101
India

Butterworth-Heinemann, Editorial Dept.
225 Wildwood Ave.
Woburn, MA 01801-2041 U.S. 1